Ephesians

40 Daily Insights by **Robert M. Solomon**

Our Daily Bread Publishing is affiliated
with Our Daily Bread Ministries.

Requests for permission to quote
from this book should be directed to:
Permissions Department
Our Daily Bread Publishing
P.O. Box 3566
Grand Rapids, MI 49501
Or contact us by email at
permissionsdept@dhp.org

Design by Joshua Tan
Typeset by Grace Goh

ISBN 978-1-913135-21-8

Printed in the United Kingdom
Second Printing in 2020

Foreword

People have many different opinions about the church, not all of them positive. To be sure, the church on earth is not perfect. But it is being perfected by the triune God, and Paul's letter to the Ephesians teaches many deep truths about how this is being done.

And it begins where we should begin—with the Father, Son, and Holy Spirit, who are all intimately involved in the life of the church and its individual believers. If not for God, there would be no salvation and no church. This truth has profound effect on the way we live. Paul makes a distinct contrast between "the ways of this world" and "the heavenly realms", where believers are seated with Christ through the grace and power of God (Ephesians 2:2, 6). This makes the church a supernaturally empowered and gifted entity that is able to show a unity and holiness that is not seen in the world. Relationships are radically changed at home, in the workplace, and in society at large. Thus the church, with its believers, becomes God's salt and light, witness and servant.

This epistle is bathed in prayer. It shows us how we can praise, thank, and trust God, and how we can pray for others even as we engage in spiritual battle ourselves. Paul's letter to the Ephesians inspires us deeply as we discover how much God loves us with the riches of His grace (1:7). It shows us how much we are "God's handiwork" (2:10), and challenges us to respond to God by loving Jesus "with an undying love" (6:24).

To God be the glory,
Robert M. Solomon

We're glad you've decided to join us on a journey into a deeper relationship with Jesus Christ!

For over 50 years, we have been known for our daily Bible reading notes, *Our Daily Bread*. Many readers enjoy the pithy, inspiring, and relevant articles that point them to God and the wisdom and promises of His unchanging Word.

Building on the foundation of *Our Daily Bread*, we have developed this devotional series to help believers spend time with God in His Word, book by book. We trust this daily meditation on God's Word will draw you into a closer relationship with Him through our Lord and Saviour, Jesus Christ.

How to use this resource

READ: This book is designed to be read alongside God's Word as you journey with Him. It offers explanatory notes to help you understand the Scriptures in fresh ways.

REFLECT: The questions are designed to help you respond to God and His Word, letting Him change you from the inside out.

RECORD: The space provided allows you to keep a diary of your journey as you record your thoughts and jot down your responses.

An Overview

The apostle Paul wrote his letter to the Ephesians from a Roman prison around AD 60 to 62. He also wrote letters to the Colossians, Philippians, and Philemon. No one knew what would happen to him as he awaited trial on trumped-up charges by opponents who hated him and his gospel preaching. Paul used the opportunity (see Ephesians 5:15–16) to write four epistles, which found their way into the New Testament.

In this letter we gaze upon the lofty heights of God's eternal plans to bless us, we marvel at Christ's work of salvation that brings life and peace to us, and we become aware of the evil days in which the saved children of light are to live faithfully. The epistle is a theological and pastoral reflection on the nature, origin, character, mission, and future of the church.

Paul begins by detailing all the blessings that the triune God has given to the church. These are found in Christ, through whom believers are made alive and given a new dignity and destiny. Jews and Gentiles are brought into one church through the barrier-breaking peace of Christ. This gospel mystery has been entrusted to the church, which is challenged to live out its identity and calling in unity and purity.

This calling involves us putting off the old life of sin and putting on the new life in Christ, leading to profound transformation in motives, behaviour, and all relationships. In this way, the church is God's new society, living amid the old sinful one as it stands its ground against the assault of hostile spiritual forces. Christ—the church's Head and Groom—will ensure that the church will be victorious and inherit its future in Him.

The structure of the book reflects these themes:

1:1–2	Salutation
1:3–23	The church's blessings from the triune God
2:1–10	The church's salvation in Christ
2:11–22	The church's unity in Christ
3:1–21	The mystery of the gospel and the church's mission
4:1–16	The united and mature church
4:17–5:21	The purity of the church in an evil world
5:22–6:9	The church and its households
6:10–20	The church's spiritual battle
6:21–24	Final greetings and blessings

Day 1

Read Ephesians 1:1–2

I f we receive a letter from someone with authority, we would pay close attention and read it many times to understand its message clearly. From the earliest days of the church, Paul's letters were considered authoritative (2 Peter 3:15–16). Ephesians begins by identifying the writer as Paul (Ephesians 1:1).

"An apostle of Christ Jesus." An apostle is a "sent one"; the title specifically designates a person who had seen Jesus and was appointed by Him. Paul states his credentials as an apostle of Christ Jesus. He did not write on his own authority and initiative, but on an authority that was given to him by the Lord. In Acts 9:15, the Lord said of Paul: "This man is *my* chosen instrument to proclaim my name . . ."

"By the will of God." Paul's appointment was in accordance with the Father's will and purpose. The phrase reminds us that the Son of God does nothing outside of or contrary to the Father's will (Hebrews 10:7). Likewise, nothing in the will of the Father excludes the Son of God—Father and Son work together in perfect unity and purpose. This means that Paul's appointment as apostle had heaven's full endorsement, and therefore enjoyed heaven's authority and resources.

The recipients ("the saints", or believers) had two addresses:

"In Ephesus." Ephesus, the capital of the Roman province of Asia Minor, was famous for its temple of Artemis, one of the seven wonders of the ancient world. It had a grand theatre, an impressive stadium, and a bustling marketplace. It was also a centre for magic and the occult (Acts 19:19). Like many cities in the Empire, Ephesus promoted sexual immorality, greed, and idolatry (Ephesians 5:3–5). It was such an important city that Paul spent over two years teaching there.

"In Christ Jesus." While the saints lived in a challenging and uncertain context, they also had a permanent address—"in Christ Jesus". This is one of Paul's favourite phrases. It means that our lives are to be centred on Christ and placed under His authority.

We too have two addresses: one temporary and earthly, the other permanent and heavenly. In this world we have trouble, but in Christ we have peace (John 16:33)—the peace that comes through divine grace (Ephesians 1:2). **The secret of living faithfully in a troubled and troubling world is to live in Christ.**

Reflect on God's call in your life. What is your attitude to this calling (or appointment), and how are you living it out?

Why is it important to remember that your permanent address is in Christ Jesus? What does it mean to live in Him? How will this help you to live faithfully and effectively in the world?

Day 2

Read Ephesians 1:3

Paul launches immediately into glorious praise of the triune God for the many blessings that the Father, Son, and Holy Spirit have showered upon the saints. In the original Greek text, Ephesians 1:3–14 come in one long and breathless but elegant sentence, without punctuation marks or pause. It is as if Paul had dived into the mystery of God's blessings and was reluctant to surface for air because he had found such stunning truths about God's rich wisdom and mercy.

Verse 3 is a summary and introduction of what follows. Our blessings from heaven have a Trinitarian basis and source: the Father and Son are clearly mentioned, while scholars have noted that the word *spiritual* points to the Holy Spirit who imparts these blessings.

The biblical doctrine of the Trinity is central to the Christian faith, yet the human mind has difficulty grasping the truth of a three-in-one God. In discussing the mystery of the Trinity, *A Handbook of Christian Truth* wisely observes: "He who would try to understand the Trinity fully will lose his mind. But he who would deny the Trinity will lose his soul."

In Ephesians alone, the Trinity is emphasised many times: 1:3, 11–14, 17; 2:18, 22; 3:2–5, 14–17; 4:4–6; 5:18–20. Scripture portrays the Trinity as working together in perfect unity in creation (Genesis 1:1–3; John 1:1), in the incarnation (Luke 1:30–35), in the redemption of sinners (Hebrews 9:14), in believers' communion with God (Ephesians 2:18), and in prayer (Romans 8:27, 34).

All three persons in the Trinity are actively working in our lives. This results in great and wonderful blessings which are described in two ways:

"In the heavenly realms." This phrase is repeated four other times in Ephesians (1:20; 2:6; 3:10; 6:12) and points to the spiritual dimension. It affirms that we have already been blessed with every spiritual blessing, although we await their full expression in heaven. Note that Paul's focus is not on physical blessings, for he describes what God has done for us through Christ in verses 4–8 and 13–14.

"In Christ." We have been blessed "with every spiritual blessing in Christ". There is no blessing outside of Christ and none apart from Him. It would be foolish to try to look for extra blessings beyond Christ.

The triune God is at work in our lives and has showered us with all the spiritual blessings found exclusively in Christ.

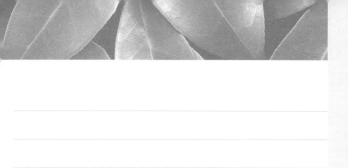

Through

Reflect on how the three persons of the Trinity are at work in your life. How do you relate to them and how should you thank them?

How does the truth that every spiritual blessing is found in Christ affect the way you live and the way you relate to Him? What does the phrase "heavenly realms" mean to you personally?

Day 3

Read Ephesians 1:4–6

I n praising the triune God for His many blessings, Paul begins with the blessings received from the Father, of which he highlights two.

Election. The Father "chose us" (Ephesians 1:4) and "predestined us" (v. 5). Paul repeats these phrases in verse 11. What do they mean? It means we are redeemed because God, in His sovereign will, has planned and determined to save us. This truth is supported by the phrase "before the creation of the world" (v. 4). We were chosen before the world began, before human beings existed. In other words, there is nothing that we have done or can do that can contribute to our salvation (see also 2 Timothy 1:9, Titus 3:5). We cannot take credit for our salvation.

We are saved entirely on the basis of what Christ has done. There is no place for a theology of works, in which we mistakenly think that we can earn our salvation. Salvation is received as a free gift of God in Christ; all that is needed is to place our trust in Christ. God has freely given us His glorious grace in Christ (Ephesians 1:6).

It also means that God was not at a loss when Adam sinned, and that His plan to save the human race was not merely an afterthought. God is never taken by surprise; He is sovereign and has full control of history and our destiny. He does everything according to His "pleasure and will" (v. 5).

God chose us so that we may be "holy and blameless in his sight" (v. 4). While our divine election is a privilege, our way of living is a responsibility made possible by God's grace.

Adoption. The Father has adopted us as His children by regenerating us (John 3:3). A baby cannot legally use his inheritance (Galatians 4:1–7), but an adopted adult son can do so. By adopting us, God has made us co-heirs with His only Son (Romans 8:17) who is the heir of all things (Hebrews 1:2). Thus, all our blessings are in Christ.

In another sense, our full adoption lies in the future (Romans 8:22–23)—when we will receive the fullness of our inheritance in Christ from the Father, who has loved us from eternity.

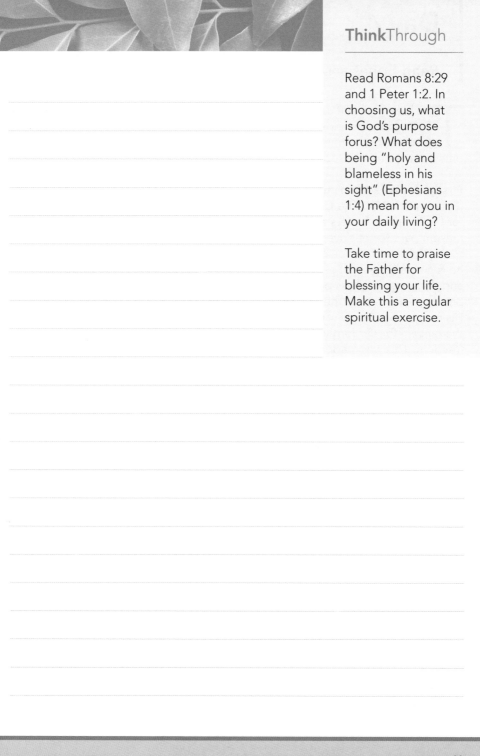

ThinkThrough

Read Romans 8:29 and 1 Peter 1:2. In choosing us, what is God's purpose forus? What does being "holy and blameless in his sight" (Ephesians 1:4) mean for you in your daily living?

Take time to praise the Father for blessing your life. Make this a regular spiritual exercise.

Day 4

Read Ephesians 1:7–12

The blessings that Jesus, God's Son, brings are closely related to those of the Father. They are gifts from the triune God.

Firstly, Jesus redeems us (Ephesians 1:7–8). The Greek word for "redemption" refers to the ransom paid to set slaves free. It is to buy an object or person so that he is not sold again. It sets free and delivers a helpless person from bondage. Jesus paid the price with His own blood, by giving Himself as the ransom for our forgiveness and freedom. This was made possible by "the riches of God's grace" (v. 7).

In Christ's sacrifice on the cross, we witness God's generous, self-sacrificing love for us. Who can grasp God's infinite wisdom and boundless mercy? We can only stand amazed at the lengths to which Jesus went to redeem us. Because of Him, we are adopted as God's sons (1:5), saved from our sins (2:5), raised up to be seated with Christ (2:6), given access to the Father (2:18), and counted as fellow citizens of God's people (2:19).

Secondly, Jesus reveals the mystery of God's will (vv. 9–10). He shows us God's mind. God's good pleasure and purpose is centred on Christ, for all history is the unfolding of God's plan to bring all things in heaven and earth under the headship of Christ (v. 10). This is where history is headed. We may not fully understand this, but we can fully believe it and experience the peace and reassurance that Christ will have the final word. In Him we are safe as part of God's wise and gracious eternal plan.

Thirdly, as God's only begotten Son, Jesus is the heir of all things (Hebrews 1:2). Because the Father has adopted us, making us Christ's brothers and sisters and God's children, we have become co-heirs with Christ (Romans 8:17). He will share His eternal inheritance—His glory—with us.

Paul also used another metaphor to describe Christ's relationship with His church: He is the husband and the church is His bride (Ephesians 5:23–32; Revelation 19:7–8). Again, this portrays how Jesus will share His inheritance with us. In fact—and amazingly—He will not claim His inheritance apart from us.

The purpose of our redemption and future inheritance is to the "praise of his glory" (Ephesians 1:12)—a phrase that concludes each section devoted to the blessings from the three Persons in the Trinity (vv. 6, 12, 14).

Jesus purchased your forgiveness and freedom with His blood. You have been lavished with God's love. Take some time to thank Him for saving you from eternal condemnation.

If you are related to Jesus, then you are related to the One who will inherit and rule all things. How can you strengthen your relationship with Him, and how will this help you live in a fallen and sinful world?

Day 5

Read Ephesians 1:13–14

The Spirit's blessings are connected with the Father's sovereign choice and the Son's redeeming work. He is the "promised Holy Spirit" (Ephesians 1:13), which we read of in Ezekiel 36:26–27: "I will give you a new heart and put a new spirit in you . . . *I will put my Spirit in you* and move you to follow my decrees".

To have God's Spirit in us, we need to be born again (John 3:5–6), or regenerated.

Jesus promised that He and the Father would send the Spirit (John 14:26, 15:26). While the Spirit does many things in us, Paul highlights two blessings:

He is the seal (Ephesians 1:13). The sealing by the Spirit occurs when someone hears and then believes the gospel. Its purpose is to:

- Show ownership (1 Corinthians 6:19–20; 2 Corinthians 1:22)

- Authenticate the believer's salvation (Romans 8:9)

- Guarantee our inheritance in Christ (Ephesians 1:14)

- Transform believers into Christ's image (2 Corinthians 3:18; Romans 8:29)

The Spirit brings unshakeable assurance (Romans 8:16) and is intimately connected with our salvation and growth in holiness.

He is the deposit (Ephesians 1:14). The Greek word for deposit can mean "down payment" or "engagement ring"—both of which effectively convey the point. In the words of theologians B. Wintle and K. Gnanakan, the Spirit is not a "monopoly" of a gifted few but "the guarantee given to all believers".

Salvation is a process. Yes, we have been saved, but we also await salvation. We were redeemed (Ephesians 1:7), are being redeemed (Romans 8:1–14), and will be redeemed (Ephesians 1:14). We are now being saved, and as we await our final salvation, we are reassured by the Spirit's presence in our lives. He is the guarantee that the good work God has begun in us will be brought to completion on the day of the Lord (Philippians 1:6). On that day, God will inherit His people as His special possession (Ephesians 1:14).

In Paul's lofty praise of the triune God working together for our salvation, he reiterates that all the redemptive activity of the three persons of the Trinity is directed towards God's glory—not our glory, but His. Thus, Paul's entire sentence of praise is centred on God and His honour. We reflect God's pleasure (Ephesians 1:6), God's purpose (v. 9), and God's possession (v. 14); by God's grace, these are all connected with our redemption and future in divine glory.

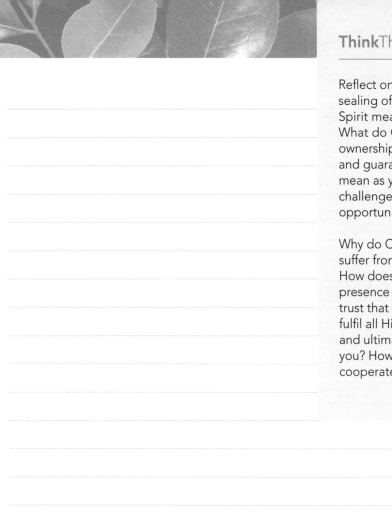

ThinkThrough

Reflect on what the sealing of the Holy Spirit means. What do God's ownership, presence, and guarantee mean as you face challenges and opportunities daily?

Why do Christians suffer from doubt? How does the Spirit's presence help you trust that God will fulfil all His promises and ultimately save you? How can you cooperate with Him?

Day 6

Read Ephesians 1:15–16

Ephesians 1 is all about God. Paul praises Him for all the blessings He has provided through Christ (Ephesians 1:3–14), then tells the Ephesians that he has been praying that they will fully understand the significance of God's gifts and grace (vv. 15–23).

In the original Greek text, each of these two sections is one long sentence, signifying that each is a comprehensive and coherent act in itself. Paul's prayer and thanksgiving are so exhilarating and intense that there are no breaks or pauses. Their appearance one after another also demonstrate the deep connection between praise and prayer—knowing who God is and what He has done, and praying in response to that sacred revelation.

Paul mentions "this reason" (v. 15), referring to his long sentence of praise for the blessings of salvation received from Father, Son, and Holy Spirit. It is because of the knowledge of God and His blessings that Paul is able to plunge into prayer for the Ephesian believers. If our knowledge of God is truly growing, we too will grow in our prayer life. Our prayer life must also be rooted in who God really is; otherwise we will be praying to an imaginary or mistaken conception of Him.

Theologian J. I. Packer's *Knowing God* gives us a classic study of God's character and relationship with us, and can help us turn our reflections into praise. **A true study of biblical doctrine is not a dry intellectual exercise, but one that flowers into praise and worship. And praise naturally flows into prayer.** This is the reason why the true theologian does his work on his knees.

Paul has heard good and encouraging reports about the Ephesian Christians. In particular, he has heard about their "faith in the Lord Jesus" (their key vertical relationship) and their "love for all God's people" (horizontal effect). As theologian and Bible teacher John Stott observes, "Every Christian both believes and loves." Paul thanks God for the Ephesians, as their Christian lives were structured well. So why does he still want to pray for them? It is because they needed to know God better and experience His blessings more deeply.

As in his praise, Paul also has a Trinitarian focus in his prayer. He prays to the Father, dwells on Christ, and refers to the Spirit. This triune God is the reason and focus of our praise and prayer.

What would happen if our worship and prayers are not well grounded in the proper doctrine and knowledge of God? How can you deepen your knowledge of God?

Paul did not cease to give thanks to God for the Ephesian believers. What lessons can you learn from that? Is there anyone you have forgotten to thank God for in your prayer?

Day 7

Read Ephesians 1:17–18

Whom do you regularly pray for and what do you usually ask God for on their behalf? The one thing Paul keeps asking God for on behalf of his fellow Christians in Ephesus is that they "may know him better" (Ephesians 1:17). Knowledge is necessary for us to grow in discipleship and holiness, as well as in character and service. Paul has two aspects of knowledge in mind.

Firstly, this knowledge is relational. Paul prays that the believers may know God better (v. 17). We are called not only to know about God (e.g. that He acts kindly towards us), but to also experience this knowledge personally.

Many Christians have only a superficial knowledge of God, like how they know their regular bus driver or postman. We pass by such people every day, but know very little about them and their personal lives. **All of us need to get to know God better by spending time with Him in reading His Word and in prayer, and by reflecting on and experiencing Him more deeply.**

Secondly, this knowledge has to do with "the hope to which he has called you" and "the riches of his glorious inheritance in his holy people" (v. 18). We can understand this by referring to Paul's praise of God (vv. 3–14).

God has chosen us, saved us, and is preparing us for something unimaginably great and noble. We are not just called *from* a sordid life of sin and a hopeless eternity of destruction, but we are also called *to* a new life, to "participate in the divine nature" (2 Peter 1:4) and to reign with Christ (2 Timothy 2:12). Why play in a muddy, sinful little puddle, pursuing the fleeting treasures and pleasures of this world, when God is calling us to a glorious ocean of divine blessings? Knowing this truth, and the fact that God has called us to be His special inheritance (Ephesians 1:18), will give us wisdom to live faithfully.

Such knowledge comes from God's revelation, which opens the eyes of our heart (our inner spiritual eyes) so that, through the Spirit, we can accept and grasp God's truth as revealed in His Word. This revelation is the product of both the Spirit's enlightenment and the careful study of (and reflection on) the Word and God's truth. They stand together.

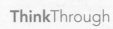

In what ways do you need to know God better? Make a list of things you can do over the next few weeks and months that will help you in your quest.

Why is it important to know the hope to which you have been called? How can you remind yourself of this hope amid the hustle and bustle of daily life and the lure of the materialistic marketplace?

Day 8

Read Ephesians 1:19–21

Besides praying that the Ephesians will come to know God better, Paul continues to pray that they will also know God's "incomparably great power" (Ephesians 1:19).

When the apostle visited and stayed in Ephesus for more than two years during his third missionary journey, believers there witnessed "extraordinary miracles" done by God through him (Acts 19:11–12). They saw God's power at work. Now, in his prayer, Paul points to even greater manifestations of God's supreme and sovereign power. These have to do with Christ.

Firstly, God's "mighty strength" raised Christ from the dead (Ephesians 1:20). Biblical scholar F. F. Bruce observed, "If the death of Christ is the supreme demonstration of the love of God, as Paul wholeheartedly believed (Romans 5:8), the resurrection of Christ is the supreme demonstration of his power".

Secondly, God's amazing power elevated Christ to be seated at His right hand (Ephesians 1:20)—a place of highest honour and authority. Jesus is there now (Romans 8:34), as "God exalted him to the highest place" (Philippians 2:9). Think of all the rulers and leaders in history, all the titles that have been given to men, and all the powers in the unseen world; Jesus has been placed in a position of authority above them all (Ephesians 1:21).

Today, these truths continue to bring comfort and encouragement to those of us who have placed our trust in Jesus. We may be suffering from old age or a crippling disease. We may be gripped by extreme poverty or persecution. We may be filled with frustration at a darkening and sinful world. But we have the assurance that the same power that raised and elevated Christ is also operating in our lives (Ephesians 2:4–6). We can close our eyes in death with the quiet assurance that God will keep His promise to raise us from the grave with that same resurrection power (1 Corinthians 6:14), and that even more glorious blessings await us.

We are also reminded that Christ, who is seated on His throne at the right hand of the Father over all authorities and powers, is presently interceding for us (Romans 8:34). He is speaking to the Father on our behalf and for our benefit. The highest authority in the universe loves you and me.

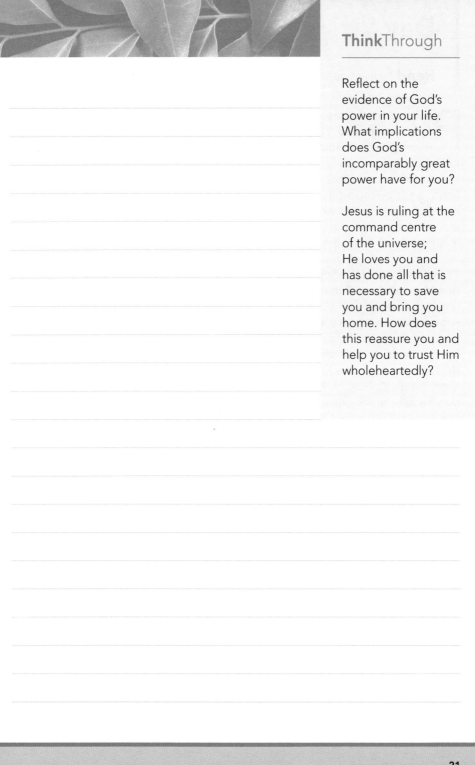

Reflect on the evidence of God's power in your life. What implications does God's incomparably great power have for you?

Jesus is ruling at the command centre of the universe; He loves you and has done all that is necessary to save you and bring you home. How does this reassure you and help you to trust Him wholeheartedly?

Day 9

Read Ephesians 1:22–23

Paul goes on to describe what God has done for His Son through His awesome power. He raised Christ from the dead, elevated Him to the throne at the Father's right hand, and "placed all things under his feet" (Ephesians 1:22). Christ's elevation above all things is in fulfilment of Psalm 8:6.

There is no created being excluded from the "all things" that are placed under the feet of Christ; He has supreme authority over all. Paul's prayer reaches its climax here as he sees Jesus at the summit of the universe. He is the "head over everything" (Ephesians 1:22)—the rightful ruler of the universe. Think of the incredibly huge universe, so large that it appears to be endless—Jesus rules over it all.

The phrase "for the church" (Ephesians 1:22) reminds us that Christ is the head of the church (4:15, 5:23), which is His body. The church has been given a Head who is no ordinary being. This head is not merely the best human being or even the most powerful angel; He is none other than the very head of the universe, the Son of God. As Bible scholar and author Arthur Skevington Wood observes, "Christ in his exaltation over the universe is God's gift to the church." What great dignity God has given to the church! Christ has authority over the church just as He has authority over the universe. It is sad that this authority is not realised or acknowledged in the world, but more so when the same thing happens in the church. Where is supreme authority placed in the church? Is it in a leader, a council of leaders, or the people? **When the authority that belongs to Christ alone is usurped and sinfully claimed or attributed to anything that belongs to the "all things" under Christ's feet, then idolatry has taken place.** Those who try to be the head will lose connection with the true Head of the church. They will suffer and cause suffering in the church (Colossians 2:19).

Not only is Christ the Head of the church, but He also fills the church with His glory and blessings (Ephesians 1:23). If Christ, in whom all spiritual blessings are found, fills the church, then the church has been unimaginably blessed indeed. What a glorious truth!

How do you think the supreme authority of Christ should be rightly expressed and experienced in church and in your heart? Who are the regular "pretenders to the throne"?

What should the world see in a church that is filled with Christ? If the world does not see this, what could be the reason? What are some solutions?

Day 10

Read Ephesians 2:1–3

Like Paul's prayer and praise in Ephesians 1, 2:1–10 is also one long sentence in the original Greek text. Paul was thinking in unbroken sentences as he plunged into the depths of God's grace and mercy, and the salvation He brought to humankind. In 1:15–23, the apostle prays that the believers would know the incomparable power of God that raised Jesus from the dead and elevated him. Here, Paul shows how God uses the same power in the believers. They too will be raised from the dead and elevated.

Paul begins by describing the past state of the believers. You were "dead in your transgressions and sins" (Ephesians 2:1), he tells them. Transgressions break God's law, while sin is falling short of God's ideal. As Bible teacher John Stott notes, "Before God we are both rebels and failures." Instead of being in Christ, in whom are found all spiritual blessings, the Ephesians were in their sins and spiritually dead. There were three things that acted against them:

First, the world. The "ways of this world" (v. 2) led them astray from God and deeper into sinful bondage.

Second, Satan. He is described as the "ruler of the kingdom of the air" and the "spirit who is now at work in those who are disobedient" (v. 2). Satan is the pretender to the throne who will be defeated by the King of kings. For the moment he is at work in unbelievers, just as God is at work in believers (Ephesians 3:20; Philippians 1:6, 2:13). It is chilling to know that Satan once had free control in us, and still tries to destabilise our lives.

Third, the sinful flesh. Paul reminds the believers that they once gratified the "cravings" and "desires and thoughts" of their "flesh"(Ephesians 2:3). Our fallen human nature colludes with Satan and the world to trap us in a terrible and debilitating bondage.

As a result, we were once "deserving of wrath" (v. 3). We were condemned to face the full brunt of God's wrath because of our sin and disobedience.

Paul reminds the believers of their previous desperate condition. New Testament scholar and theologian C. F. D. Moule reflects: "They must be led to look down again into the pit, into the grave, from which grace called them out and set them free." **It is good to remember our past, lest we forget and take our salvation for granted.**

Read John 17:14–19. How did Jesus pray for protection for His disciples against the world and Satan, and for their sancti-fication (victory over their sinful nature)? What implications are there for you?

Why is it helpful to look into the pit from which we have been saved? How will it help us to worship God and take discipleship seriously?

Day 11

Read Ephesians 2:4–7

Verse 4 begins with "But because". "But" refers to how God has intervened in our sorry state of affairs. "Because" points to the motivation behind this intervention—His great love for us. It is amazing, and a reason for our eternal wonder, that God would have such love for unlovely objects of wrath as us.

Three more words are used to describe the manner in which God has treated us: mercy (Ephesians 2:4), grace (v. 5), and kindness (v. 7). Mercy is when we are spared what we deserve (punishment). God is "rich in mercy", forgiving us even when we rebelled against him and deserved eternal condemnation. Grace is when we are given what we do not deserve. God has granted us so many blessings in Christ, none of which we deserve. And kindness is shown in how God has acted towards us in Christ (v. 7). We are undeserving of all the wonderful ways in which God has treated us.

There are also three things that God has done in our lives for which we must forever be grateful. These are the three verbs in the long sentence (vv. 3–10). Firstly, God has "made us alive with Christ" (v. 5), even as we were once dead and helpless in our transgressions and sins. We were regenerated by the grace, mercy, and power of God and made into new persons (2 Corinthians 5:17). Then "God raised us up with Christ and seated us with him in the heavenly realms" (Ephesians 2:6). Pastor and Bible teacher A. W. Tozer observes that in Christ, human nature is "received, embraced, welcomed, and enthroned at the right hand of the Father".

Each of these actions was done in association with Christ. They refer to the key events in the life of Christ: resurrection, ascension, and session (His rule from the right hand of God). **Christ has pioneered a new story for humankind so that we no longer need to be trapped in the old story.** He is our Forerunner (Hebrews 6:20 ESV). This story of Jesus becomes our story when we place our faith in Him and are united with Him. We do not deserve this one bit, but such is the magnanimous and marvellous love of God, whose gracious and merciful treatment of us will be the talk of the universe "in the coming ages" (Ephesians 2:7).

Reflect on these words: love, mercy, grace, kindness. What do they tell you about the way God has treated you? Turn your thoughts into an act of worship.

Why is it necessary to be united with Christ (Romans 6:5) in order to receive all the blessings in Him? How are you nurturing your union with the Saviour? How does His story become your story?

Day 12

Read Ephesians 2:8–10

Having spelt out what God has done for us in His mercy and grace—made us alive, raised us up, and seated us with Christ—Paul reiterates an important truth about our salvation: "For it is by grace you have been saved, through faith" (Ephesians 2:8). We are saved from the death, bondage, and condemnation mentioned in 2:1–3 entirely by God's grace. Our salvation—our rescue from death, slavery, and judgement; our new life; and our glorious eternal future—is not our own doing but the gift of God (v. 8). We have done nothing to contribute to our salvation, and are totally indebted to God.

Because this salvation is God's gift, we receive it by faith, by trusting in Christ and God's promises in Him. Even this faith is a gift from God (Philippians 1:29): we are enabled by God's grace to place our faith in Christ (1 Timothy 1:14). All the more are we eternally indebted to God for saving us.

We are not saved by our works (Ephesians 2:9); there is no one who can boast about his salvation save in the mercy of God. Our best efforts at righteousness are "like filthy rags" (Isaiah 64:6). In Bible teacher John Stott's words, we "shall not be able to strut round heaven like peacocks". Instead, "heaven will be filled with the exploits of Christ and the praises of God".

Our salvation in Christ is an accomplished fact. We have been saved; the Greek verb is in perfect tense, meaning that we can have the full confidence that our salvation is fully secured.

Paul concludes by declaring that "we are God's handiwork" (Ephesians 2:10); the Greek word means poem or work of art. Truly we can offer nothing to God in His transformation of us. **Salvation is not an improvement but a new creation, not a repair job but a total overhaul.** Also, though good works cannot save us, we are saved to do good works. God has planned all this from eternity and has saved us accordingly. Because of God's grace, instead of walking in our sins (v. 1), we can now walk in our good works (v. 10).

Why does religion tend to degenerate into a belief system based on works? Why is it important to maintain in both thinking and practice that we are saved entirely by God's grace? Reflect on your own life in this regard.

We are saved to do good works. What does this mean for you? Who do you think should receive credit for any good work that others may see in you?

Day 13

Read Ephesians 2:11–13

God's work of salvation is not confined to the Jews; it extends to all peoples. This truth of God's mission to save the nations is embedded deeply in the Old Testament (Genesis 12:3; Isaiah 56:7) and made clear in the New Testament (Ephesians 3:1–6). Paul reminds the Gentile Christians of their previous state ("you who are Gentiles", Ephesians 2:11); it should have made them shudder just thinking about it. They were:

- Separated from Christ
- Not counted as God's chosen people
- Not entitled to the rights and privileges God gave to His chosen people
- Without hope
- Without God

To be separated from Christ is to be excluded from all spiritual blessings. To be excluded from God's people is to be deprived of the promises, rights, and privileges He has given. **To live without hope and God in this world is a most terrifying fate.** Bible scholar William Hendricksen summarised the pre-conversion spiritual condition of the Gentiles: they were "Christless, stateless, friendless, hopeless, and Godless".

We too were in such a desperate situation (whether we realised it or not) before we turned to Christ. We were alienated from God and His people. That was our condition "formerly" (v. 11), and it is good for us to remember that in order to fully appreciate the tremendous divine grace that has radically reversed our state of affairs.

Paul then moves to the "now" (v. 13) and reminds his Gentile brethren how they have been "brought near" (v. 13) to God and also to the Jews. This has been achieved "by the blood of Christ" (v. 13). There is no other way we can come near to God. Jesus himself emphasised this when He said: "No one comes to the Father except through me" (John 14:6).

Paul also declared in other letters that there is only one mediator between God and alienated men—Christ, who died as a ransom for all (1 Timothy 2:5–6). Through His death, Christ has brought us near to God. Though we were once alienated from God, we are now reconciled with Him and have peace with Him (Romans 5:1).

John Stott, in pointing out the two phrases "in (or by) the blood of Christ" and "in Christ Jesus",

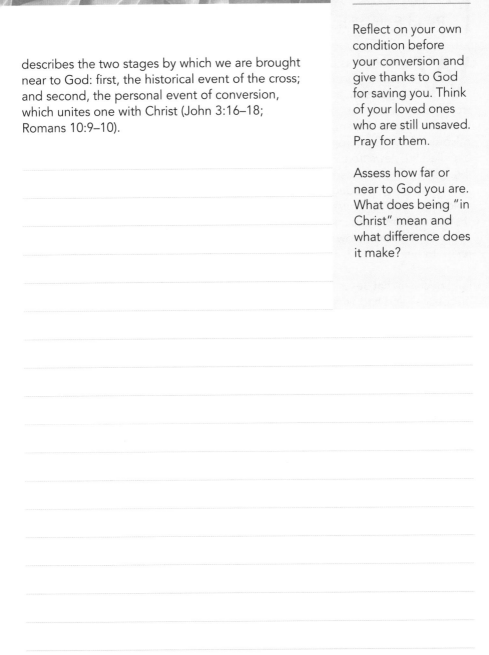

describes the two stages by which we are brought near to God: first, the historical event of the cross; and second, the personal event of conversion, which unites one with Christ (John 3:16–18; Romans 10:9–10).

Reflect on your own condition before your conversion and give thanks to God for saving you. Think of your loved ones who are still unsaved. Pray for them.

Assess how far or near to God you are. What does being "in Christ" mean and what difference does it make?

Day 14

Read Ephesians 2:14–18

What Christ has done brings us near to God as well as to one another. In the ancient world, there was an unbridgeable gap between Jews and Gentiles. Gentiles despised Jews (Emperor Claudius expelled the Jews from Rome in AD 49), while Jews considered Gentiles as fuel for hell. Now, through the Spirit's guidance and Paul's missionary efforts, there were both Jews and Gentiles in the early church. How should they relate to one another?

Paul declares that Jesus "himself is our peace" and had "made the two groups one" (Ephesians 2:14). "For through him we both have access to the Father by one Spirit" (v. 18). Not only is this verse Trinitarian—pointing to the unity in diversity we find in the Trinity—but it also points to how the Gentiles and Jews in the church are to be united through the peace that Christ brings.

There was a thick barrier—a "dividing wall" of hostility—between Jews and Gentiles: they hated each other. One of the expressions of this barrier was the law of Moses that the Jews practised. But now, Christ "has destroyed the barrier . . . by setting aside in his flesh the law with its commands and regulations" (vv. 14–15).

But did Jesus not say that He came not to abolish the law but to fulfil it (Matthew 5:17)? We can explain this apparent discrepancy by noting that the law mentioned in Ephesians 2:15 refers to the ceremonial law, while Matthew 5:17 refers to the moral law.

The observance of the law (by which Jews hoped to be saved) was an impossible task for Jews and a foreign concept to Gentiles. **By abolishing the law that separated them, Jesus made it possible for both Jews and Gentiles to be reconciled with God.** He also made it possible for them to be reconciled with each other, now that they had a common way of salvation in their common access to the Father (Ephesians 2:18). It is in this way that Christ preached peace to those near and far (v. 17).

God's purpose is to create a new humanity, a new society, and a church comprising both Jews and Gentiles (v. 15), both of whom have been reconciled to God through the cross as well as to each other, and to destroy the ancient hostility between them. Our salvation has significant social implications.

What is the significance of Christ abolishing the law with its commands and regulations? How does it affect salvation for all?

What sinful barriers in society are carried into the church? How can the truth of Galatians 3:28 be lived out in the church? Can you personally do anything about some of these barriers?

Day 15

Read Ephesians 2:19–22

Many of us live in highly individualistic modern societies. Even Christians see their salvation in very individualistic ways—me and my God, me and my salvation. But that is a faulty way of thinking. While the Christian faith must be personal, it must not be private; it has social ramifications.

Paul elaborates on how God acts to save us by reconciling us with Him and also with one another. In His ancient plans are blueprints for a new society—the church. Ephesians 2:11–22 introduces three sections with the key words "formerly" (v. 11), "but now" (v. 13), and "consequently" (v. 19). **The salvation that brings people near to God and one another has great consequences, which Paul describes in a way that brings purpose and dignity to the church.**

Although the Christian faith was built on the older Jewish faith, Gentile Christians were not second-class citizens in the church. They were "fellow citizens with God's people and also members of his household" (Ephesians 2:19). Thus the status of the Gentiles before their conversion (v. 12) was reversed. Paul describes the church as a kingdom and a family in which Gentiles and everyone else had full citizenship and membership.

The church was also a building established on Christ and His teachings. By faithfully propagating Christ's teachings, the apostles and prophets had set the foundations in obedience to the Lord. These teachings would later become the Holy Scriptures; hence the unique authority of Scripture in the church. All teachings and prophecies find their meaning and fulfilment in Jesus, and thus He is the chief cornerstone upon whom the church is raised and held together (vv. 20–21).

Today, there are no apostles and prophets with such foundational roles and authority. But we are all part of this building ("living stones", 1 Peter 2:5), built and held together in Christ. He is the unifying Head, and in Him we rise up to be a living temple for the Lord, in which we all serve as priests (Hebrews 13:15; 1 Peter 2:5).

The church is the new temple (made not of stones and mortar, but of people), the dwelling place of God (Ephesians 2:22). This is a wonderfully high view of the church that needs to be recovered through the recommitment and submission of the church to its living Head.

ThinkThrough

The church is a kingdom, a family, and a temple. How do these truths affect the way you and your fellow church members relate to God, one another, and the world?

Believers in church are "joined together" and "built together" (Ephesians 2:21). How should this be experienced and how can it be strengthened?

Day 16

Read Ephesians 3:1–6

After explaining the wonderful work of God in reconciling us to himself and to one another, Paul moves on to pray for the Ephesians. "For this reason" in 3:1 refers to the gospel truths set out in Ephesians 2. But Paul interrupts himself, continuing his prayer only in verse 14. In between he plunges again into a discussion of the great "mystery of Christ" (Ephesians 3:4); he was so enthralled by it all.

Paul uses the word "mystery" several times (3:3, 4, 6, 9; 5:32). This refers not to an unsolvable conundrum or a secret, but to a hidden truth (v. 5) that is now revealed. This mystery was made known to Paul "by revelation" (v. 3). It was not a philosophy or social strategy that Paul developed on his own, but something God had told him about.

"This mystery is that through the gospel the Gentiles are heirs together with Israel, members together of one body, and sharers together in the promise in Christ Jesus" (v. 6). For many centuries, the Jews—to whom God had revealed Himself and His law—saw God as the exclusive deity of Israel. They failed to recognise that He was the God of all nations and that He intended to extend His salvation to

them all. Their narrow and restrictive thinking reduced God to a tribal god in their minds.

It is not that Scripture did not disclose God's global intentions (Psalm 67:1–2; Isaiah 19:23–25); rather, this truth was hidden from previous generations (Ephesians 3:5) in that the Jews never understood it. The prophet Jonah, who was sent to Nineveh, failed to understand God's global mission. **Even more radically, the mystery is about the coming together of Jews and Gentiles into one church. This aspect was unknown before**. But now, this mystery "has now been revealed by the Spirit to God's holy apostles and prophets" (v. 5; Ephesians 4:11–12; 1 Peter 1:10–12; 2 Peter 1:19–21).

For this reason, Paul was appointed by God to be an apostle to the Gentiles. He was now in a Roman prison but he considered himself not a prisoner of Caesar or of unfortunate circumstances, but of Christ (Ephesians 3:1). He knew he was ultimately in the hands of Jesus. He was a prisoner *of* his Lord and *for* the Gentiles. He was totally committed to Christ and the gospel mission.

Imagine how it must have been for Paul to learn about the mystery of Christ. How would it have changed his worldview and life direction? Do you see something similar in your life?

How willing are you to be a prisoner of Christ (Ephesians 3:1; Philemon 1:9; 2 Timothy 1:8)? What factors may prevent you from becoming one?

Day 17

Read Ephesians 3:7–13

Paul marvels at the profound mystery revealed to him, as well as at his appointment as a "servant of this gospel" (Ephesians 3:7). He was a strict Pharisee, "a Hebrew of Hebrews" (Philippians 3:5) who took pride in his Jewishness. He was the least likely candidate to be the apostle to the Gentiles. But God's choices often defy human wisdom, logic, and strategy (1 Corinthians 1:27).

Moreover, Paul considers himself as "less than the least of all God's people" (Ephesians 3:8). When writing the letter to the Galatians—which came some years before his epistle to the Ephesians—Paul showed that he was an apostle equal to the others, even Peter (Galatians 1:1, 2:11). But now, he uses humble words. The longer he lives and serves Christ, the more he is amazed and humbled by God's grace. In the words of preacher Charles Spurgeon, "The fuller a vessel becomes the deeper it sinks in the water". The more fruit a branch bears, the lower it hangs.

Paul's ministry was totally dependent on God for its success. It was given to him by God's grace and performed through God's power (Ephesians 3:7). He knew what he had to do. He was to "make plain to everyone" what God was doing ("administration" is "plan", ESV) now that God had revealed it to him (v. 9). Though the gospel carried the "boundless riches of Christ" (v. 8), the preacher's task was to use plain speech so that people could understand. That is something we need to remember on the pulpit and in the classroom.

God's plan is larger than we can imagine. He wants to use the church (where Jew and Gentile are brothers and sisters) to teach the "rulers and authorities" (angelic beings in the heavenly realms) a lesson (vv. 10–11). They will marvel at God's manifold wisdom—that He brought together fallen, warring, and hate-filled human beings into a beautiful body of Christ. As Bible scholar John Alexander Mackay put it, "the history of the Christian church becomes a graduate school for angels".

Paul wraps up his thoughts by encouraging his readers not to worry or be discouraged by his imprisonment (v. 13). God had the upper hand and would fulfil His eternal purpose. (Paul wrote four great epistles from the prison, Ephesians being one of them). He reminds them to pray, noting that in Christ, we have access to God and can speak freely and confidently in prayer (v. 12).

Do you think the
church has failed
to be "a graduate
school for angels"?
Has there been a
point in history when
the church may
have succeeded
in impressing the
angels?

Why is it important
that the more
successful you are
in God's work, the
more humble you
must be?

Read Ephesians 3:14–19

Paul returns to where he left off in verse 1 and begins to pray. "For this reason" probably refers to the contents of Ephesians 2 as well as 3:12 (we have prayer access to God through Christ).

The apostle kneels before the Father and marvels that His whole family is one, derived from His name and extending across heaven and earth. God's wisdom, grace, and power are indeed stupendous in forging one family out of such disparate and divided individuals and nations.

The prayer is Trinitarian. Paul prays that the Father will strengthen the "inner being" of the believers with the power of the indwelling Spirit (Ephesians 3:16). God has limitless and glorious riches from which He can do this. **What God does inside us forms the basis for what He then does through us.** Many Christians ignore what is on the inside and live out only an external and ritualistic kind of religion.

When God strengthens us through His Spirit, it leads to our hearts becoming the dwelling place for Christ, who lives (in Greek, this means "permanently reside") in us (v. 17). The life of Christ will then be seen in and through us. We will experience Christ's marvellous love, although we will never fully sound its depths. We can spend an eternity discovering how wide (He died for all), how long (eternal), how high (beyond the reach of any foe), and how deep (reaching down to the most depraved) His love for us is (v. 18). These four dimensions are interrelated and bring out the perfect love of Christ.

Indeed, this love of Christ "surpasses knowledge" (v. 19). Paul marvels at how God's divine love, which leads us into right relationships with Him and one another, is far superior to any human knowledge or religion.

Paul prays that the believers would be deeply rooted (like a tree) and grounded (like a building) in this love (v. 17) and thus be "filled to the measure of all the fullness of God" (v. 19). This is the goal. We know we are full of God when we are full of His love (1 John 4:8). This is Christian maturity, both for individuals as well as the church ("together with all the Lord's holy people"; Ephesians 3:18).

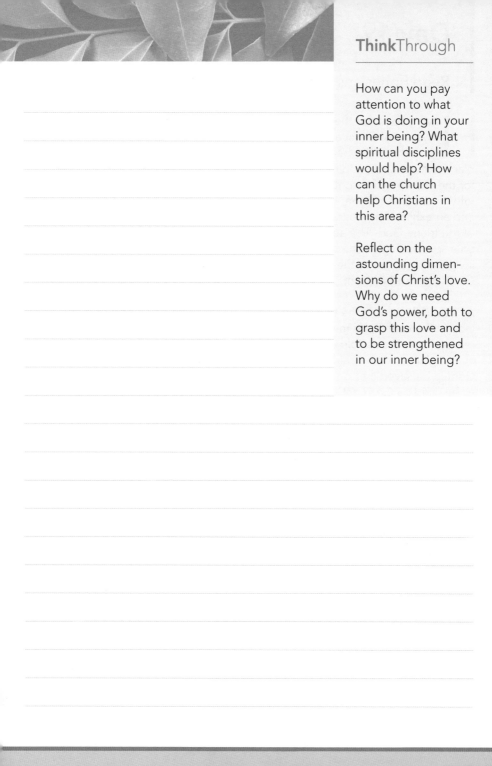

How can you pay
attention to what
God is doing in your
inner being? What
spiritual disciplines
would help? How
can the church
help Christians in
this area?

Reflect on the
astounding dimen-
sions of Christ's love.
Why do we need
God's power, both to
grasp this love and
to be strengthened
in our inner being?

Day 19

Read Ephesians 3:20–21

Having spelt out the glorious mystery of Christ and His gospel and the beauty of God's plan for the church, and having prayed for the church in the context of God's lofty truths and mission, Paul breaks into an exhilarating doxology in praise of the triune God. The apostle was on a spiritual high as he breathed the invigorating truths of the gospel and God's manifold wisdom.

As Paul reflected on the fullness of God in the church, he must have realised how impossible it all seemed at first glance. How could Jew and Gentile be saved into one church to be filled by God? Yet this was possible because God is able to do infinitely more ("immeasurably more", Ephesians 3:20) than we care to ask in prayer or can even imagine in our private thoughts. As Bible commentator Adam Clarke put it, God is able to do "superabundantly above the greatest abundance". God has planned this from eternity and "his power that is at work within us" (v. 20) is able to accomplish this. Only God can do this.

Paul wants to glorify God. Charles Spurgeon observes that Paul could not say, "Unto him be glory in my soul" because "his one soul afforded far too little space, and so he cried 'Unto him, be glory in the church'". Paul possessed a bird's eye view of God's grace and its effects on the church in the universe. He understood its significance, and was therefore able to see the glory of God in the church.

Paul also sees God's glory "in Christ Jesus" (v. 21). Earlier we saw that the mystery of Christ had to do with the bringing together of Jew and Gentile into the one church of God. In Ephesians 5, we see another aspect to this mystery—the bringing together of the church and Christ, the body and its Head, the bride and her Groom (5:32). This is indeed a mystery, as we reflect with great wonder on how it is possible for God and humankind to be united in such an intimate fashion.

To see God's glory in Christ and in the church is to recognise this mystery.

This glory is an everlasting glory— "throughout all generations" and "for ever and ever" (v. 21).

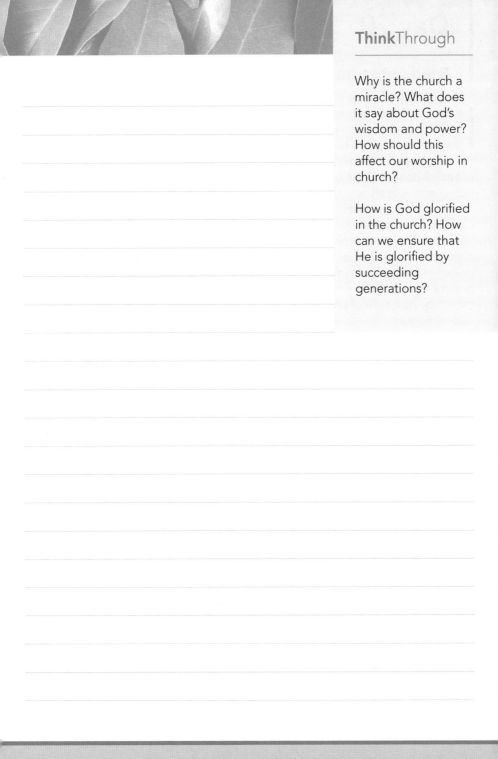

ThinkThrough

Why is the church a miracle? What does it say about God's wisdom and power? How should this affect our worship in church?

How is God glorified in the church? How can we ensure that He is glorified by succeeding generations?

43

Day 20

Read Ephesians 4:1–3

In the first three chapters, Paul dwells on lofty doctrines and reflections, prayer and praise as he plumbed the depths of God's love, the heights of His wisdom, and the unimaginable power that is at work in the church. We have been given beautiful views of salvation and the church, the new humankind, and the new society created by divine grace, mercy, and power. In reality, however, we know that the church is often not what it should be, because of unbelief and disobedience.

So, in the next three chapters, Paul turns to practical issues. It is a wonderful demonstration of the connection between doctrine and discipleship, between language and life, between principle and practice. "Therefore" (Epehsians 4:1 ESV) Paul urges his readers to "live a life worthy of the calling you have received" (v. 1). Our calling is full of splendour, as seen in the grandeur of the first three chapters, which must be matched by our individual and community life. God's grace will enable us to live according to His plan and purposes.

After all that God has done, after all that Christ has sacrificed on the cross, after all the gifts and the power the Spirit has given to the church, it would be a great tragedy if the church did not reflect the beauty of the bride of Christ. One of the signs of the loveliness of Christ's church is unity. We are not called to create this unity (through proper management strategies and team building games, perhaps), for it is already given to the church. It is the "unity of the Spirit" (v. 3), who sanctifies us and fills us with God's truth and love. The problem arises when we disrupt and discard what has been given to us through pride and other sinful attitudes.

For the church to stay united, it is necessary that believers make "every effort" to preserve that unity and peace (v. 3). Every member must pull together in the same direction under the leadership of the Spirit and in the strength of the Lord. For this to happen, godly attitudes such as humility, gentleness, and patience—all based on godly love—are necessary (v. 2). We are to spare no effort—"Be *completely* humble and gentle" (v. 2)—and remember that there is always room for improvement.

Why do the church and Christian individuals not live up to the plans and resources of God? Ask this question of yourself as well.

Why is Christian unity received rather than created (or manufactured)? How have you contributed to Christian unity both positively and negatively? Reflect on verse 2 and pray for its presence in your life.

Day 21

Read Ephesians 4:4–6

Unity should mark the church that was purchased by the blood of Christ. Though the church comprises diverse peoples (Jews and Gentiles), it is one. This unity is not the same as uniformity, where there are no differences.

One look at the global church today will reveal many differences—different ethnic groups, contexts, languages, church structures, issues, and concerns. However, the church of Jesus Christ has a basic underlying unity that is far more important than all the differences and provides a way of dealing with them.

Here, Paul emphasises how the church is to be "one". Note that our oneness is rooted in the oneness of the triune God. This passage is Trinitarian: one God and Father (Ephesians 4:6), one Lord (v. 5), and one Spirit (v. 4). Though there are three Persons in the Trinity, they are one (John 10:30) and they act together as one. The Trinity is the source and the standard for unity in the church.

Jesus prayed to the Father for all believers to be "one as we are one" (John 17:22). The Lord had a great vision for His church as He prayed that

His followers would be "brought to complete unity" (John 17:23). Such unity is possible only through the grace and power of the triune God.

Paul mentions the Father who is "over all and through all and in all" (Ephesians 4:6). The "all" refers to the believers. We worship the same God who rules over us all, have the same salvation experience as the same God works within us, and are united in a common mission and ministry as He works through us all. This is how the church experiences unity.

The unity in the church is doctrinal ("one faith and hope"; common beliefs and values), liturgical ("one baptism"; common traditions and rituals), and corporate ("one body"; we function organically as one).

Why do Christians quarrel over minor and unimportant differences when they have so much in common? We worship the same God and Father who is at work in us, and we share the same resources He has given so generously. We should celebrate and live out this unity so that the world may believe Christ (John 17:23).

ThinkThrough

The Trinity is the source and standard for unity in the church. What does this mean and what implications are there for the church?

Make a list of what is common in all churches. How does focusing on what we have in common help us deal with our differences?

Day 22

Read Ephesians 4:7–13

Unity does not mean there is no place for God-given diversity in the church. Built upon the underlying unity of the church are the many spiritual gifts bestowed. As Paul wrote, we all "form one body" and "have different gifts" (Romans 12:5–6).

There are different passages in the Bible that speak of spiritual gifts and gifting (Romans 12:6–8; 1 Corinthians 12:8–10, 28–30; Ephesians 4:11; 1 Peter 4:11). In this passage, the focus is on people endowed with special abilities by the Spirit, whom Christ gave as "gifts" to the church. Their purpose is for the growth of the church.

These are important gifts to the church, each person receiving special "grace" (enablement or ability) as determined and apportioned by Jesus (Ephesians 4:7) for the different church offices. "It was he who" gave to the church apostles, prophets, evangelists, pastors, and teachers (v. 11).

Based on the Greek text, many scholars consider pastor-teacher as one gift. Some also note that while apostles and prophets were necessary in the early church in order to establish Scriptural foundations, they may no longer be operative today—at least not in the same way they were in Paul's time. One important practical principle remains in the church, however, and it is that gifts and offices must be matched properly.

Note that it is Jesus who decides who is gifted in what way. Paul adapts Psalm 68:18 to depict Jesus as the ascended Lord (after He descended to earth and won a great victory) who sovereignly gave gifts to men (Ephesians 4:8–10). Elsewhere we read that the Spirit decides on the gifts (1 Corinthians 12:11) and that the Father decides on the appointments (1 Corinthians 12:28). There is no contradiction or confusion here, for it shows that Father, Son, and Holy Spirit work together in unison. And it provides a model for how all spiritual gifts must be put together for a common purpose.

That purpose is building up the body of Christ, "until we all reach unity" and maturity, "attaining to the whole measure of the fullness of Christ" (Ephesians 4:13). This will be expressed both in Christian service (v. 12) and in a growing knowledge of Christ (v. 13). **This is how ministry should be focused— on facilitating deeper intimacy with Christ and effective and faithful service for Him, carried out by all.**

Christ apportions grace and gifts to His disciples. What do you think He has called you to do, and how has He gifted you? How are you fulfilling this calling?

Reflect on Christian unity and maturity. How are they related? How does focusing on knowing Christ contribute to unity? Why is maturity connected with the fullness of Christ?

Day 23

Read Ephesians 4:14–16

The combination of unity and maturity in Christ produces a lovely church that is truly the body of Christ.

Continuing his reflection on unity in the faith and maturity in Christ, Paul goes on to describe what will happen when these qualities are missing or weak. The church will then be deceived and distracted; Christians will be like immature, unstable infants, and their faith will be tossed about by the currents of false and alluring teachings (Ephesians 4:14). Deceitful teachers will lead gullible people astray. **Like the wind and waves, false teachings produce a lot of motion (and emotion), but no real growth and progress in the Christian life.**

Sadly, there are many examples of this today. Unbiblical teachings, Christ-less activism, superficial emotionalism, and the focus on religious trivialities are all serious obstacles to spiritual maturity.

A church that is growing in unity and maturity provides an altogether different picture. Such a church grows in its connection with its Lord. In all things, the believers "grow to become in every respect the mature body of him" (v. 15). He is the head of the body, and it is He who provides unity and maturity in the church. "From him the whole body" is held together strongly and grows up in love (v. 16). Without Christ, we cannot be united or grow into maturity. As Charles Spurgeon observed, "A church that is only united in itself, but not united to Christ, is no living church at all". The phrase "whole body" refers to a unity that requires participation by all.

One key characteristic of this unity and maturity is love. We cannot claim to have unity and maturity if we do not have love (1 Corinthians 13). It is in this godly love that we are built up (Ephesians 4:16). It is with this love that we learn to speak the truth (v. 15), never compromising, but always communicating it in God's love. It is also with this same love that we perform our God-given work in the body of Christ and in the world. A sign of unity and maturity is that each member of the church will do his or her part (v. 16) for the glory and honour of God.

What forms of superficial Christianity can you see today? How is the lack of unity and Christian maturity connected with this?

As we grow up into Christ, we will find unity and maturity. How can we do this? Why is love a key manifestation of unity and maturity? How should it be expressed in your life?

Day 24

Read Ephesians 4:17–24

From the glorious heights of the heavenly places (Ephesians 1–3) to the promising potential of the church (Ephesians 4:1–16), Paul now descends to the reality of the sinful world.

The church is in this world, but this world must not be in the church. The believers in Ephesus were gathered by God into the redeemed church. They were to make a clean break with their past and no longer live like unbelievers (v. 17). Society in Ephesus and in the ancient Roman Empire was filled with spiritual darkness, moral impurity, and sexual immorality. It was an environment that was hostile to Christian living.

Worldly people have hardened hearts (v. 18) that are unable and unwilling to respond to God. This keeps them in spiritual ignorance. They are thus separated or alienated from God and His life, and do not understand truth. As a result, all their thoughts ultimately amount to nothing. The result of going down this ungodly path is that its travellers lose "all sensitivity" to the things required by God and give themselves over to "sensuality", or moral impurity and sexual immorality (v. 19). Bible commentator William Barclay points out that a licentious man "does not care how much he shocks public opinion so long as he can gratify his desires". What was true in Ephesus is also true today.

A follower of Christ must live a radically different kind of life ("That, however, is not the way of life you learned", v. 20). Christians "heard about Christ" (v. 21) and were "taught in him" (v. 21). **Christian education and intimacy with Christ help us to live differently. This involves putting off the old self and putting on the new self—a "self transplant".**

The old self is the sinful nature, the instrument of our "former way of life" that is "corrupted by its deceitful desires" (v. 22). The new self is God's new creation of the regenerated self; it is "created to be like God" (v. 24). This new nature within us enables us to be holy and righteous as we trust in Christ and allow the Spirit to do His sanctifying work in us (1 Peter 1:2). Without this "self transplant" performed by God in us, we cannot live as Christians or live in heaven.

Reflect on Paul's description of our "former way of life". Do you see any aspects of this sinful way of life still present in how you live today? What will you do about it?

Some people have not taken off the old self completely. Some have not put on the new self properly. How would you assess your own progress in putting on your new self?

Day 25

Read Ephesians 4:25–28

Believers are called to discard our old selves and put on our new selves. This has significant implications for our behaviour and relationships, as conveyed by the word "Therefore", which links the previous section with this section (Ephesians 4:25). In the next few verses, Paul looks at some examples of transformation that will be seen in us when we are regenerated and have put our old selves on the cross.

There are three areas in which radical transformation can be seen. Each has to do with one of the Ten Commandments: the ninth (Exodus 20:16), the eighth (20:15), and the sixth (20:13). With each example, Paul continues to apply the idea of "putting on" the new self and "putting off" the old self.

Firstly, each believer is urged to put off falsehood and speak truthfully to his neighbour (Ephesians 4:25): there should be integrity in his speech, communication, and relationships. The reason—"for we are all members of one body"—is that if the various parts of our body practise deceit when they communicate with one another, we will have a sick, confused, and paralysed body. How much more true this will be in the church, where we are to speak the truth in love (v. 15).

Secondly, we must avoid sinning when we get angry (v. 26). Becoming angry is a visceral response and we may not be able to prevent it, but what we do next determines whether we sin or not. **Anger must be quickly dealt with in a godly way and must not be allowed to linger over to the next day.** To harbour anger and bitterness is to allow the devil to gain a foothold in our lives. The devil is happy to provoke our anger to boiling point or to let it simmer for a long time and thus destroy our souls; anger is like acid that harms the vessel in which it is stored. Jesus revealed the connection between nursing anger and murder (Matthew 5:21–22).

Thirdly, he who used to steal must stop (Ephesians 4:28). People steal for various reasons, such as laziness and greed. The transformed believer must now work (no more laziness) and from his wages share with those in need (no more greed). This illustrates the "putting off" and "putting on" concept. We are not only to renounce sin, but also to pursue goodness.

ThinkThrough

Consider how people avoid speaking truthfully, e.g. speaking only about inconsequential matters. Why is telling the truth important for the health and maturity of the church?

Why do people enjoy nursing their anger? Why is it important to deal quickly with anger, and how does this reflect the character of God (Psalm 30:5)?

Day 26

Read Ephesians 4:29–32

These verses continue to outline the challenge issued in the preceding section—that the transformed life should be obvious to all. Again, Paul deals with the tongue, described by James as "a world of evil among the parts of the body" that often "corrupts the whole body" (James 3:6). "It is a restless evil, full of deadly poison" (James 3:8).

Jesus taught that it is not what goes into a man's mouth but what comes out of it that makes a man unclean, because it is the output of an unclean heart (Matthew 15:11, 18–20). He also warned that we will be judged for every careless word, and that the total output of our speech will acquit or condemn us (Matthew 12:36–37).

"Unwholesome talk" includes vulgarity, slander, and contemptuous speech. This must be replaced by wholesome speech that builds up and encourages (Ephesians 4:29).

Putting off the old self includes getting rid of "all bitterness, rage and anger, brawling and slander", and "malice" (v. 31). Anger can explode into rage or freeze into bitterness. Brawling and slander are the works of a quarrelsome person, and malice is the result of evil in the heart. These are the works of the old man and have no place in the Christian's life.

Instead, the believer must put on kindness, compassion, and a forgiving heart. The new man must treat others the way God has treated him. He must not be like the unmerciful servant who, having been forgiven an enormous debt by his kind master, went on to treat his fellow servant— who owed him a much smaller debt—harshly (Matthew 18:21–35). God has forgiven us "for Christ's sake" (Ephesians 4:32 KJV). Charles Spurgeon advises those who find it difficult to forgive another to do it at least for Christ's sake.

Kindness and forgiveness are characteristics *modelled* after God; we are *motivated* by Christ and *enabled* by the Spirit who produces this godly fruit (Galatians 5:22–23) in us.

When we fail to put off the old man and his sinful manifestations and to put on the new man, the Holy Spirit with whom we were sealed is grieved (Ephesians 4:30). John Stott notes that the indwelling Spirit is grieved by anything that is "incompatible with . . . purity or unity" that comes from God and should characterise Christians.

Read Proverbs 10 and reflect on the characteristics of "the mouth of the righteous" and "the mouth of the wicked/fool" (vv. 11, 14). What personal lessons have you learned?

Consider situations in an individual Christian's life as well as in the church that would bring sorrow to the Holy Spirit.

Day 27

Read Ephesians 5:1–2

Before proceeding to discuss the transformed Christian life, Paul touches on a central dynamic of this life.

Christians are called to be "dearly loved children" of God (Ephesians 5:1). Those who receive Jesus as their Saviour and Lord by believing in Him become God's children (John 1:12). To be a child of God is to be born of the Spirit—that is, to be regenerated by God's Spirit into becoming a new person in God's Kingdom and a member of God's family (John 3:5).

If we are God's children, then we will have a family resemblance. We will look like the Son of God who is the perfect image of the Father (John 14:9). God has called us and "predestined (us) to be conformed to the image of his Son" (Romans 8:29) so that we will share the family resemblance and be like our heavenly Father—especially in character.

It is in this sense that we are called to "follow God's example" (Ephesians 5:1). We are to be exact copies of Him in that we are to be perfect like our perfect heavenly Father (Matthew 5:48).

God's perfection was seen in Christ, His only begotten Son. Jesus loved us fully with His self-sacrificial love. He "gave himself up for us as a fragrant offering and sacrifice to God" (Ephesians 5:2). There is no greater love than giving in self-sacrifice for others (John 15:13). Jesus, as our Good Shepherd, laid down His life for us (John 10:11). The Father sacrificed His only Son so that we may be saved (John 3:16). Every time we look at the cross, we see how much the Father and Son loved us.

Paul emphasises that we must now "live a life of love, just as Christ loved us" (Ephesians 5:2). **Our lives must be characterised by that same self-giving love that we received from God. We do this by imitating Christ.**

There is, however, a difference between imitation and mimicry. Circus animals can be trained to imitate human actions but only externally—this is mimicry. Imitation, on the other hand, copies not only external behaviour but also internal motivation. In this sense, only those who are truly born again, who have the Spirit of God in them, and whose eyes are constantly on Jesus, can imitate God.

Think about how churchgoers may try to mimic Christ without really having a relationship with Him. Why is it important for you to be a child of God before you can truly imitate God?

The quality of our love must be the same as that of Jesus—"As I have loved you, so you must love one another" (John 13:34). What are the implications of this in your life?

Day 28

Read Ephesians 5:3–7

Ephesus was a centre for many things. Like many pagan cities in the Mediterranean world of the first century, it was a centre of idolatry, which was often associated with temple prostitution. Society then was permissive in sexual matters, and sexual immorality was common and tolerated—in some cases, even celebrated. Greed was also common; Ephesus had many wealthy people with big houses. It was a commercial centre that profited from being an idolatrous city of sex.

The readers of Paul's letter were used to living and thriving in such a sinful environment. But now they were to be different: they must resist the temptations and renounce their former way of life. Paul makes a list of things that must not be tolerated among Christians—there "must not be even a hint" of these sinful practices (Ephesians 5:3).

The list includes sexual immorality and greed. Impurity includes obscene and dirty talk. Such things are "improper for God's holy people" (v. 3) and "out of place" (v. 4). Paul warns: "No immoral, impure or greedy person . . . has any inheritance in the kingdom of Christ and of God" (v. 5). Why? Because such practices are contradictory to life in the church and in heaven. God's children must not live like the children of the world. They must be different precisely because they are the children of God, who is holy.

Instead of immorality and greed—which is idolatry, because it is the worship of material things above God to gratify one's desire (v. 5; see Matthew 6:24)—God's children are to be known for their habit of thanksgiving (v. 4). Gratitude to God will help believers stay away from immorality, impurity, and greed.

Today, Christians live in a hyper-sexed and greed-driven world. How can they live as God's children? **Christians must remember their true identity and stay away from anything that is incompatible with being God's children.** They must not allow themselves to be deceived by "empty words" (v. 6), whether these come from loud and misleading advertisements, or irreverent gossip in the social media. They must remember that God's wrath will come upon the disobedient, and must therefore not be partakers (v. 7 KJV) with those who embrace such sinful lifestyles and habits. Rather, they should be partakers of the divine nature (2 Peter 1:4).

ThinkThrough

How important is the Christian identity? What are some modern habits, experiences, or places that are connected with immorality, impurity, and greed? How can you resolve to have nothing to do with these things?

How can you reach out to those imprisoned in the sins that are rampant in this world, without getting caught in those sins? How would you make your Christian principles and values clear to them?

Day 29

Read Ephesians 5:8–17

Continuing his "putting off, putting on" paradigm, Paul contrasts light and darkness. In Christ we are now light (New Testament scholar Peter T. O' Brien notes that at conversion, it is our lives, and not our surroundings, that are changed from darkness to light); we should therefore renounce the darkness that was once inside us (Ephesians 5:8).

Because of our new identity in Christ, we are to walk as children of light by bearing the "fruit of the light" (v. 9; the same as the fruit of the Spirit, Galatians 5:22–23). There is no place for the "fruitless deeds of darkness" in the Christian's life (Ephesians 5:11). Such disobedient deeds are shameful and we should develop a distaste for them (v. 12).

Light exposes darkness (vv. 13–14), and God's light exposes the sinful deeds of darkness. So we cannot say we don't know about the shameful deeds of darkness. Rather, as we receive the light of Christ that shines on us (v. 14, may be an adapted quotation of Isaiah 60:1 or an early hymn), we are able to unmask dark deeds in us and others. In God's light we can see sin for what it is and stay away from it. The key outcome is: "Have nothing to do with the fruitless deeds of darkness" (Ephesians 5:11).

Rejecting darkness and putting on light involves finding out "what pleases the Lord" (v. 10) and understanding "what the Lord's will is" (v. 17). Discovering and doing God's will is central to Christian discipleship. Firstly, it is a sure test that one is a child of God (Mark 3:35; Matthew 7:21; 1 Peter 4:2). Secondly, it involves being "filled with the Holy Spirit" (Ephesians 5:18, instead of being drunk with wine—again in line with the idea of "putting off, putting on"). The Spirit helps us to do God's will. Not knowing God's will is foolishness (v. 17); knowing it but not doing it is equally foolish (Matthew 7:26).

Though we are surrounded by evil, knowing God's will helps us to redeem every good opportunity and live with practical godly wisdom (Ephesians 5:15–16). Sin is not only the wrong that we commit, but also the good that we fail to do when we have an opportunity. We must therefore live carefully (v. 15), not carelessly, so that we will not only know God's will but also follow it every day.

ThinkThrough

How does Christ shine on us? As light and darkness are incompatible, what implications are there for the Christian when dealing with situations where lines are blurred and values may even be reversed?(see Isaiah 5:20)

How do you discover God's will for your life, and how seriously do you aim to obey it? Biblical imperatives like those listed in 1 Thessalonians 4:1–3, 5:16–18 provide a framework for God's general will. Reflect on them.

Day 30

Read Ephesians 5:18–21

We have the Word and the Spirit to help us live as children of light. Together, the Word (that helps us know God's will) and the Spirit (who enables us to understand the Word and do God's will, Philippians 2:13) assist us in walking in the light.

We are commanded to be filled with the Holy Spirit—and not be drunk with wine which leads to excessive indulgence. The Greek verb in verse 18 translated as "filled" is a present imperative: this implies that being filled is to be a consistent lifestyle, not just a one-time experience.

Being filled with the Spirit enables us to do four things (Ephesians 5:19–20). Firstly, we can have true fellowship when we "speak to one another with psalms, hymns and spiritual songs" (v. 19). Secondly, we can truly worship when we make music in our hearts to the Lord. Thirdly, we can pray gratefully, giving thanks to God for everything. And fourthly, we can submit to one another. Here is the true bride of Christ in action.

Notice that the call for mutual submission is not to be misunderstood in terms of modern notions of egalitarianism—it is to be done out of reverence (or fear) for Christ (v. 21).

The Greek word for submission contains an idea of orderliness. As John Stott points out, biblical submission is a "humble recognition of the divine ordering of society". It is often misunderstood when we take the perspective that everyone is equal in every respect. That Paul did not mean this, is clear from his discussion of relationships in the family and workplace: he speaks of husband-wife, parent-child, and master-slave (or servant) relationships. In these, there are some who have been given authority which must be respected. But the authority must not be abused.

People in such relationships are of equal worth in God's eyes, but they have different roles and responsibilities. As theologian John H. Yoder observed, "Equality of worth is not identity of role". **We must avoid unbalanced interpretations of what Paul says, whether in thinking that some are inferior to others, or in believing that there is no God-instituted hierarchy in social relationships.**

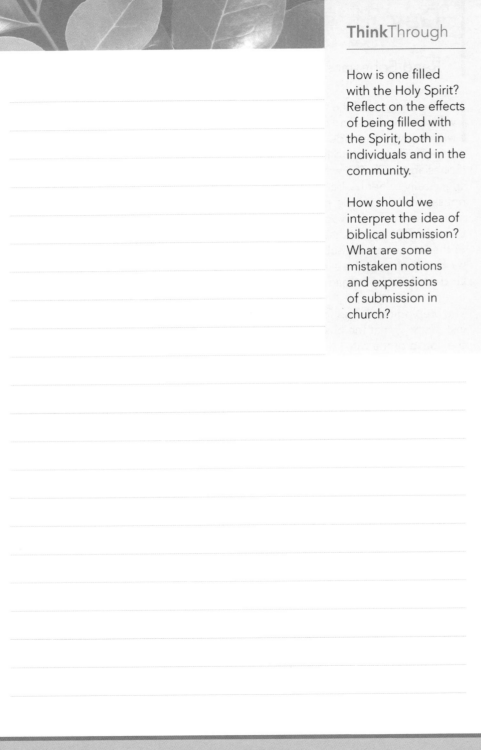

How is one filled with the Holy Spirit? Reflect on the effects of being filled with the Spirit, both in individuals and in the community.

How should we interpret the idea of biblical submission? What are some mistaken notions and expressions of submission in church?

Day 31

Read Ephesians 5:22–24

In his discussion of the husband-wife relationship, Paul begins with the wife's attitude to her husband. The key word is submission (Ephesians 5:22). The wife is to submit specifically to her husband; Paul does not say that she should submit to all men. The phrase "as you do to the Lord" (v. 22) suggests that she submits to the Lord when she submits to her husband—that is, she accepts the God-made order in marriage.

The theological reason for this instruction is that the husband is the "head of the wife" (v. 23). The model for this is the headship of Christ over the church. In the same way that Christ is head of the church, the husband has spiritual authority over his wife. Some may recoil at this, seeing it as a case of ancient patriarchy or male chauvinism. But Paul uses a theological argument, which means this is not merely a cultural view confined to specific cultures or historical periods.

God instituted marriage, and though both man and woman are made in His image and are equal in dignity and essence (Genesis 1:27, 5:1–2; Mark 10:6), He also established an order in which the husband has spiritual authority (1 Corinthians 11:8–10). Sin has marred this relationship, which often results in power struggles between husband and wife (Genesis 3:16).

The statement that the husband shall rule over the wife (Genesis 3:16 NLT; 1 Corinthians 14:33–35; 1 Peter 3:1–6) is not prescriptive but descriptive of the consequences of sin—husbands will tend to bully their wives because of their physical and social advantage, while wives will often fight back, seeking to control their husbands in some way. The word "desire" in Genesis 3:16 is the same Hebrew word used in Genesis 4:7, where sin is described as seeking to master Cain. In other words, sin has turned marital relationships into battles for dominance.

However, in Christ the marital relationship is redeemed and made new (1 Corinthians 11:11–12; Galatians 3:28). It can now be viewed in terms of divine love: the wife loves her husband as she submits to her husband "in everything", just as the church does with Christ (Ephesians 5:22). In so doing she shows her love for her husband and her Lord.

What is God's order for marriage? How has this been affected by modern ideas and practices?

How can spiritual authority be abused? Is the church submitting to Christ? What lessons can we l earn from this for marriage?

Day 32

Read Ephesians 5:25–33

The key word describing the husband's responsibility is love: "Husbands, love your wives" (Ephesians 5:25). The husband's authority is not to be abused but exercised in love. He must not lord it over his wife, but love her in a self-giving way. The model is Christ's love for the church—"just as Christ loved the church" (v. 25). Jesus expressed this self-giving love in the following ways (vv. 25–27):

- He gave himself up for the church (by dying for her).

- He makes the church holy (sanctifies) by washing her with water through God's Word.

- He will present her to himself as a "radiant church, without stain or wrinkle or any other blemish, but holy and blameless" (v. 27). This will take place at the marriage supper of the Lamb, when He comes again (Revelation 19:6–9).

As the husband is not Christ, he cannot do for his wife all that Christ did for the church, such as sanctifying her or washing her of her sins, nor is he required to do so; verses 25–27 focus on Christ. But the husband must show the same kind of selfless love, and even be willing to give his life for his wife. This challenges any notion of abuse of power and authority in a marriage. The way of Christ is the way of love, and the husband is to follow His example. Christ showed His love in the past, is showing it in the present, and will show it in the future. This divine love is consistent and lasting ("undying love", Ephesians 6:24).

The second model for marital love looks at how a man loves and cares for his own body (Ephesians 5:28–29). A man ought to love his wife as he does his own body. Again Paul points to Christ and notes the way He treats the church, His body (vv. 29–30). Adam and Eve became "one flesh" (one body) through marriage (v. 31; see Genesis 2:24), so a man's wife becomes like his own body, which he is to care for and love.

Marriage as instituted by God has a more profound meaning than we often realise. The "mystery" (Ephesians 5:32) compares the relationship between husband and wife to that between Christ and the church. Just as Christ loves the church, the husband loves his wife. And just as the church obeys Christ, the wife submits to the husband. **When a man and a woman obediently fulfil their duties to each other, their marriage reflects the relationship between church and Christ.**

Paul concludes by summarising the main point: a husband must love his wife and she must respect (submit to) him (v. 33).

Reflect on how Christ loves the church. What does it say about how husbands ought to love their wives? What are the implications for your own life?

How do people love themselves—in the right way? How can a husband love his wife "as he loves himself" (Ephesians 5:33; Matthew 22:39)?

Day 33

Read Ephesians 6:1–3

Paul now moves on to another familial relationship—that between parents and children. This is the second of three sets of relationships examined in the light of the call for submission (Ephesians 5:21) that results from being filled with the Spirit. We have already seen that submission is to be performed according to the order established by God, and should arise from reverence (or fear) of Christ.

In describing each set of relationships, Paul begins with those who are to submit to the other (wives, children, and slaves) before moving to the other party, who must approach the relationship with responsive and responsible love.

In the case of parent-child relationships, children are to obey their parents (6:1). This obedience is further described as being "in the Lord" and "right" (v. 1). This is the order established by the Lord and is correct regardless of culture and era.

Jesus himself demonstrated it when He was 12 years old. Luke 2:41–51 recounts how His parents had left Him in Jerusalem without realising it when they headed home. When they returned to the city to search for Him and found Him at the temple, Mary was cross with Him. Jesus explained that He had to be in His Father's house, but His parents did not understand what He meant. Nevertheless, Jesus went home with them "and was obedient to them" (Luke 2:51). Jesus obeyed His parents because it was the right thing to do; it reflected God's order.

The fifth commandment to honour one's father and mother (Exodus 20:12) is the only commandment that comes with a promise—long life in the Promised Land. God blesses those who obey Him. It is not that we are saved by obeying, but that we are saved to obey (1 Peter 1:2, 22). The Old Testament prescribes capital punishment for the child who curses or hurts his parents (Exodus 21:15; Leviticus 20:9) or disobeys them (Deuteronomy 21:18–21). This shows how seriously God views the matter.

Today, it is increasingly common to see children disobeying their parents and openly showing disrespect. Elder abuse is on the rise. The breakdown in parental authority mirrors the breakdown in many other forms of God-ordained authority. **Our challenge is to encourage all children to follow Christ's example by obeying and respecting their parents and God's order.**

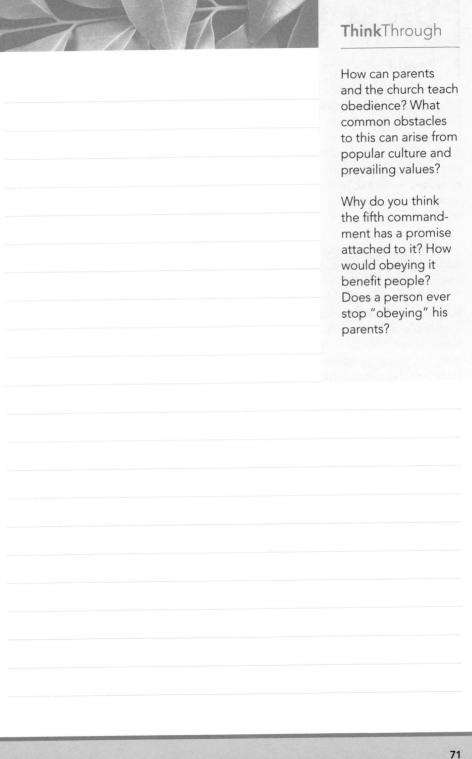

How can parents and the church teach obedience? What common obstacles to this can arise from popular culture and prevailing values?

Why do you think the fifth commandment has a promise attached to it? How would obeying it benefit people? Does a person ever stop "obeying" his parents?

Day 34

Read Ephesians 6:4

In the parent-child relationship, the parent has been given the authority. That is God's order for a healthy family and society. Like in all other relationships, such authority must be exercised with responsibility and care; it must not be abused, nor should the trust be betrayed.

Continuing the concept of putting off the old self and putting on the new, Paul instructs fathers not to "exasperate" their children, but to train and instruct them about the Lord (Ephesians 6:4). This command is meant not only for fathers but also mothers, just as children are to obey both their fathers and mothers.

What do fathers need to put off? Fathers are to avoid exasperating their children. Some translations use the phrase "provoke to anger" (or wrath). When fathers are abusive, it will result in deep resentment and anger in their children. This can in turn lead to violent and dysfunctional behaviour. The parent must not bully the child simply because he has the power and authority over the child. It is a reminder for parents today not to vent their anger and daily frustrations on their children.

Uncontrolled anger, especially when combined with efforts to discipline the child, can do more harm than good. Bible teacher Martyn Lloyd Jones rightly points out that a parent, before disciplining his child, must have first controlled himself. He asks, "What right have you to say to your child that he needs discipline when you obviously need it yourself?"

What do fathers need to put on? Fathers should train and instruct their children. The Greek word for "train" is also translated as "discipline". Both training and instruction are functions of Scripture (2 Timothy 3:16), and parents are to fulfil their responsibilities to guide their children in the ways of God. Both discipline and teaching are needed in order for this to be effective, and the methods need to be modified for different age groups.

Responsible parenting means bringing up and nourishing children so that they grow "in wisdom and stature, and in favour with God and men" (Luke 2:52; 1 Samuel 2:26; Luke 1:80). At a time when couples choose not to have children for various reasons and when parental love seems to be increasingly missing or marred, Paul's instructions remind us of God's blueprint for healthy family life, as well as the importance of nurturing the young for the future.

ThinkThrough

Reflect on your own experience as a child. What good and bad experiences did you have? How have these affected you and your own parenting style?

How can discipline and teaching be combined for children of different ages? How can the church encourage stressed-out parents to devote time and attention to good, responsible parenting?

Day 35

Read Ephesians 6:5–8

Slaves were an important part of Roman society. In cities such as Ephesus, up to a third of the population was made up of slaves working in households and serving not only as domestic servants but also as teachers and physicians. Slaves had minimal rights and faced the ever-present threat of abuse and oppression.

Paul did not condone slavery; neither did he lead a revolution against it. But as illustrated in his epistle to Philemon, Paul encouraged Christians living in a society that had institutionalised slavery to act in a Christian manner so that the system could be replaced by a more equal and just society. Paul's approach, as New Testament scholar C. F. D. Moule put it, was "not to batter but to undermine". There were many slaves in the early church, and for Paul to address them before their masters would have been a radical move in itself.

Slaves are to submit to their masters in deference to God's order ("as you would obey Christ", Ephesians 6:5). They may have hated their masters, especially if their masters were demanding or cruel, and served grudgingly or cut corners in their work. The Greek word in verse 6, translated as "when their eye is on you", is literally "eye-service". Slaves who hated their masters would work hard only when the boss was around, perhaps just to score brownie points.

For the Christian slave, all this was to change because of Jesus. Each of Paul's specific instructions to slaves focuses on Christ. They should obey their masters just as they would obey Christ (v. 5). They should serve as "slaves of Christ" (v. 6). They should serve wholeheartedly as if they were serving Christ (v. 7). And they should always remember that it is the Lord who will reward (and punish) everyone, slave and master alike (v. 8). This core relationship with Christ would make the Christian slave radically different.

The Christian slave would obey and respect his earthly master, provide sincere and diligent service, and seek to do God's will from his heart. As John Stott put it, he would have a "higher preoccupation" amid his more mundane tasks (v. 6). Such a slave would serve his earthly masters well because in his heart he was serving the heavenly Master. He would be a great witness to his master that his heavenly Master "did not come to be served, but to serve" (Mark 10:45).

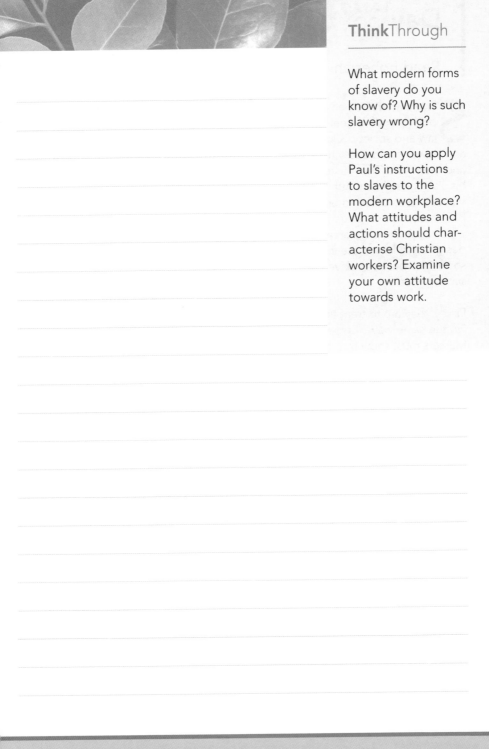

What modern forms of slavery do you know of? Why is such slavery wrong?

How can you apply Paul's instructions to slaves to the modern workplace? What attitudes and actions should characterise Christian workers? Examine your own attitude towards work.

Day 36

Read Ephesians 6:9

Slave owners had an advantageous position guaranteed by Roman law and society. Such authority and power could easily be abused, and often was. The master could beat his slave or sell him. But Christian masters were called to be different. Paul issues three instructions to them, which John Stott observes "were designed to lessen the cultural and social gap between slave and slave-owner".

Firstly, they are to treat their slaves "in the same way" (Ephesians 6:9). Masters must show the same sincerity and diligence in the way they treat and manage their slaves, just as their slaves seek to do the same in their service to their masters. Masters must provide what is "right and fair" in the eyes of the Lord, and show the respect that they expect from their slaves. Respecting slaves as persons of worth would prevent a master from abusing his slave (Philemon 1:16). If a master expects his slave to be godly, then he too should show that same godliness and fear of God.

Secondly, they should not threaten their slaves, withholding their food or rest, or worse. This instruction is consistent with Paul's argument that in all relationships where authority resides in one party, the authority must be wielded in fear of the Lord and with love.

Thirdly, the earthly master must remember that he has a heavenly Master, the same Master who has responsibility for the slave. If he ill-treats his slave, he has to answer to the slave's heavenly Master one day. He must also account to that same Master for his own conduct and life. The true Master shows no partiality, and in His presence the slave and his earthly master will stand on equal footing. Hence, knowledge of the future judgement should moderate the master's attitude and actions.

Paul's instructions to earthly masters are equally applicable to employers and bosses today—a time when the profit motive drives some employers to abuse their workers or push them beyond humane limits. **Bosses must remember that the person with authority in a relationship must exercise it with great responsibility and love, as much as the other person must respect God's order and submit to authority.**

All parties should be motivated by love, respect for God's order, and fear of God.

How might modern employers abuse their workers or treat them as less than human? How should a Christian employer treat his employees?

How should the truth that God is the supreme Master over all, and before whom we must all stand one day, affect our day-to-day relationships? Is there someone you should be treating more fairly?

Day 37

Read Ephesians 6:10–13

Paul now directs our attention back to the heavenly realms (Ephesians 6:12). This is where he started out in his letter, when he stressed that all our blessings from God are in Christ in the heavenly realms (1:3).

At the beginning of his letter, he showed that Christ is seated at the right hand of the Father in the heavenly realms (1:20), and by God's grace and power, we too are seated there (2:6). Paul then brought his discussion "down to earth" to show how, in the light of what God has done for us, we should live and how the church should manifest both unity and purity in all relationships. The apostle now moves back up ("Finally", v. 10) to the heavenly realms, where a spiritual battle is taking place.

In the heavenly realms are "rulers", "authorities", "powers", and "spiritual forces" (v. 12). These are spiritual forces allied with Satan and battling against God and the church. The list introduces us to strong forces of darkness, and a rather frightening army. But we must also remember that Jesus is enthroned above this diabolical army (1:20–21), having disarmed them at the cross (see Colossians 2:15). We must thus be neither presumptuous (for "our struggle is not against flesh and blood", v. 12) nor fearful.

We are asked to be "strong in the Lord" (v. 10), for His mighty power will deal with the forces of evil. We should stand our ground. Note the repeated use of the word "stand" (vv. 11, 13, 14): the image is that of a Christian army which stands faithfully as it does God's will.

Satan's forces will attack and his schemes include what Bible commentator E. K. Simpson calls the "twofold infernal policy" of "intimidation and insinuation". **With iron fist and velvet glove, Satan will attempt to destabilise the church, but the church must stand her ground against the charge of the enemy.** She must do this by relying on God's might and strength and by putting on the "full armour of God" (vv. 11, 13).

This armour is a spiritual one. As we wear the *full* armour, we will be completely protected against the wicked spiritual powers. This is all the more urgent because the days are evil (vv. 13; 5:16)—we cannot afford to be complacent or presumptuous.

Do Christians take seriously the threat of spiritual forces that are at work against the church? If not, why? What are the dangers of going to the other extreme and being obsessed with fear of evil forces? What would constitute a biblical posture towards evil powers?

Why is it necessary to put on the full armour of God? How does this underline the truth that we must fight the spiritual battle with God's strength and might? What does standing our ground entail?

Day 38

Read Ephesians 6:14–17

Paul must have looked at his Roman guards and used their military armour to explain the spiritual armour he had in mind. He also mentions the pieces of armour in the order a soldier would put them on. The point is that God has given us spiritual resources to protect us fully against the enemy. With this spiritual armour, we can continue standing in battle. But we must put on the *whole* armour.

The belt holds all the pieces together. It represents God's truth (Ephesians 6:14) as found in the Bible and as proclaimed in the gospel. Where there is "truth decay" in the church, there will be spiritual casualties in battle.

The breastplate protects the vital organs and is another important part of the armour. It represents righteousness (v. 14). What protects us is not our own experiences or feelings—not, as preacher Martyn Lloyd Jones put it, "the breastplate of experiences"—but the righteousness of Christ. If we have this objective protection from God, Satan cannot wound us.

"Combat boots" for the feet represent the evangelistic readiness to proclaim the gospel of peace (v. 15). The church that is ready to go out with the gospel message is in a far safer position than one that is sluggish and living in its own well.

The shield of faith (v. 16) protects us against the flaming arrows of the enemy. The material of the shield is able to not only stop the arrows, but also put out the fire. Our faith in Christ does the same.

The helmet of salvation (v. 17) protects us against doubt and other forms of attack, such as discouragement and fear. Satan can discourage us by turning up the heat of the battle, leading us to despair and wonder if victory will ever come. But God has promised to save us: we can trust Him even if our present circumstances look bad.

The sword of the Spirit (v. 17) is the only offensive part of the armour, and is clearly identified as the Word of God. Jesus is our model when He overcame Satan's attacks and temptations by using God's Word (Matthew 4:1–11).

We can stand our ground by wearing God's armour fully, from head to toe, and relying on all that God has provided us for the spiritual battle. He has not left us defenceless.

Reflect on the way you are wearing God's armour. Is there any part that is missing or wrongly worn? What actions do you need to take to ensure that you have full protection?

The shield of faith should be taken up in "all circumstances" (Ephesians 6:16 ESV). When do Christians neglect to do this? Why is faith important for all situations? (see Romans 14:23)

Day 39

Read Ephesians 6:18–20

Prayer must become a pervasive reality in spiritual warfare. It is through prayer that we move to the battleground and gain God's strength and mighty power. And it is through prayer that we secure victory, because prayer connects us with the victorious Lord.

The underlying importance of prayer is seen in the word "all", which is used four times in the ESV version of verse 18. We are to pray "at *all* times in the Spirit, with *all* prayer and supplication . . . keep alert with *all* perseverance, making supplication for *all* the saints" (Ephesians 6:18 ESV). The Lord also warned his sleepy disciples at Gethsemane: "Watch and pray so that you will not fall into temptation" (Matthew 26:41). Watchfulness ("be alert", Ephesians 6:18) and prayer go together and are both essential in spiritual battle, for a sleepy army is a vulnerable one.

The Spirit assists us in our prayers ("pray in the Spirit", v. 18; Romans 8:26–27). We are reminded that both the Spirit and the Son are interceding for us (Romans 8:27, 34). When we pray, we are united with them. That is why one of poet and hymn writer William Cowper's hymns goes:

And Satan trembles, when he sees
The weakest saint upon his knees.

We are to pray with "all kinds of prayers and requests", to "always keep on praying", and to pray "for all the saints" (Ephesians 6:18). **Prayer is a central action in spiritual warfare because it builds on the central spiritual relationship—our relationship with God.** Praying for all fellow believers, meanwhile, brings protection for all. The spiritual shield we use covers not only ourselves, but others standing with us.

It is with this in mind that Paul asks for prayer for himself (v. 19). He was in a Roman prison as Christ's "ambassador in chains" (v. 20). He was awaiting trial, yet his prayer request was not about his personal circumstances; he did not mention release from prison nor his personal comfort and needs. Instead, he asked for prayer that he would proclaim the gospel fearlessly (vv. 19, 20). At his trial, he wanted to claim the promise of the Lord—that words would be given to him (v. 19; see Matthew 10:19–20). The gospel dominated Paul's thinking even as he faced death.

ThinkThrough

Reflect on the way
Paul uses the word
"all" when referring
to prayer. What
implications are
there for your prayer
life? Is there an "all"
to which you need to
give more attention?

What should your
prayer requests be
when others ask how
they can pray for
you? How and what
are you praying for
on behalf of others?

Day 40

Read Ephesians 6:21–24

Paul concludes his letter with a personal note and a benediction. He mentions Tychicus, possibly his scribe. A native of Asia Minor (Acts 20:4), Tychicus was a younger fellow worker whom Paul trusted and often used as a messenger (Acts 20:4; Colossians 4:7; 2 Timothy 4:12; Titus 3:12). He was linked with Trophimus, an Ephesian (Acts 21:29), and could have been an Ephesian too.

Paul entrusted Tychicus with his letters for Ephesus and Colossae from Rome (Colossians 4:7–8). He had high regard for the man he called a "dear brother" and "faithful servant in the Lord" (Ephesians 6:21; Colossians 4:7). Tychicus was to tell the Ephesians "everything" so that "you also may know how I am and what I am doing" (Ephesians 6:21). He was sent to deliver Paul's personal greetings and news and to encourage the recipients of the two letters. Such personal links and communication in the early church helped to unite the believers in love and in their mission.

In his benediction, Paul uses four words that he has been emphasising in the letter to the Ephesians: peace, grace, love, and faith (vv. 23–24).

Grace and peace were mentioned in his opening greeting. God's grace makes salvation possible and results in peace in the heart, church, and home. Faith is how we respond to God's grace and is connected to love. Paul has already taken us to the heavenly realms to show us how much God loves us and how much Christ loves us, His church. And he has urged us to live with this divine love, expressing it in all our relationships as we love God and others.

Paul uses the phrase "undying love" (v. 24) to express the quality of love the saints in Ephesus have for the Lord Jesus. It is therefore sad, that we will later hear the Lord telling the Ephesian church, near the end of the first century, that "You have forsaken the love you had at first" (Revelation 2:4). **The quality of our love for God may decline if we are not careful. We must always be connected with the triune God.** Thus Paul ends the letter by mentioning the Father and the Lord Jesus, and the undying love that is a fruit of the Spirit.

ThinkThrough

What does this passage say about the quality of relationships between God's workers and churches in the early days of the church? How can this quality be recovered and maintained today?

Reflect on the words: peace, grace, love, and faith. How did Paul focus on them in the letter? How can we love the Lord Jesus with an undying love? How would this strengthen and enrich the church?

Going Deeper in Your Walk with Christ

Whether you're a new Christian or have been a Christian for a while, it's worth taking a journey through the Bible, book by book, to gain a deeper appreciation of who Jesus is and how we can follow Him.

Let faithful Bible teacher be your tour guide and help you draw closer to Christ as you spend time reading and reflecting on His Word.

Our Daily
Bread
Journey
Through
Series®

JourneyThrough®

Luke

62 Devotional Insights by **Mike Raiter**

Our Daily
Bread
Journey
Through
Series®

JourneyThrough®

Acts

50 Devotional Insights by **David Cook**

Our Daily
Bread
Journey
Through
Series®

JourneyThrough®

Matthew

62 Devotional Insights by **Mike Raiter**

JourneyThrough®

Mark

62 Devotional Insights by **Robert M. Solomon**

JourneyThrough®

John

50 Devotional Insights by **David Cook**

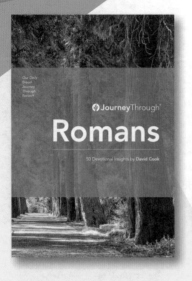

Our Daily
Bread
Journey
Through
Series®

*Journey*Through®

Romans

50 Devotional Insights by David Cook

Our Daily
Bread
Journey
Through
Series®

*Journey*Through®

Galatians

30 Biblical Insights by Khan Hui Neon

Our Daily
Bread
Journey
Through
Series®

*Journey*Through®

Colossians
& Philemon

30 Devotional Insights by Mike Raiter

Our Daily
Bread
Journey
Through
Series®

*Journey*Through®

1&2
Timothy

50 Biblical Insights by Robert M. Solomon

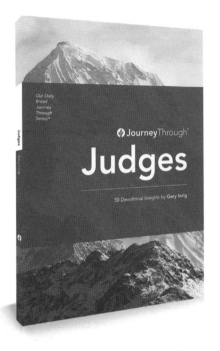

Journey Through

Judges

The book of Judges describes a low point in the history of God's people. It tells of a time of moral and spiritual anarchy, when everyone ignored God's life-giving laws and did what they thought was right in their own eyes. It is a story of disobedience and defeat. Yet the book also contains glimpses of the Israelites' capacity for greatness— when they chose to trust and depend on God. Discover God's great principles of life, and find out how we can lead powerful, productive lives in a society that is increasingly hostile to our faith.

Gary Inrig is a graduate of the University of British Columbia and Dallas Theological Seminary. An established Bible teacher and former pastor, he has authored several books, including *True North*, *The Parables*, *Forgiveness*, and *Whole Marriages in a Broken World*.

Journey Through

Hosea

As God's spokesman, Hosea is told by Him to marry Gomer, a prostitute, and to go again and again to woo her back despite her many infidelities. Hosea's commitment to love Gomer gives us a glimpse of God's love for us. God loves His people as passionately and as jealously as a devoted husband loves his wife. Even when we wander from Him and our hearts cool towards Him, He continues to come after us and to draw us back to Him. God's love will never let us go. Rekindle your love and commitment to the One who loves you!

David Gibb is the former Vicar of St. Andrew's Church in Leyland and Honorary Canon of Blackburn Cathedral. He is committed to training church planters and gospel workers, and is one of the contributors to a new NIV Study Bible. He is also author of a book on Revelation.

Sign up to *Journey Through*

We would love to support you with the *Journey Through* series! Please be aware we can only provide one copy of each future *Journey Through* book per reader (previous books from the series are available to purchase).

If you know of other people who would be interested in this series, we can send you introductory *Journey Through* booklets to pass onto them (which include details on how they can easily sign up for the books themselves).

☐ **I would like to regularly receive the *Journey Through* series**

☐ **Please send me ____ copies of the *Journey Through* introductory booklet**

Just complete and return this sign up form to us at:

Our Daily Bread Ministries, PO Box 1, Millhead, Carnforth, LA5 9ES, United Kingdom

Here at Our Daily Bread Ministries we take your privacy seriously. We will only use this personal information to manage your account, and regularly provide you with *Journey Through* series books and offers of other resources, three ministry update letters each year, and occasional additional mailings with news that's relevant to you. We will also send you ministry updates and details of Discovery House products by email if you agree to this. In order to do this we share your details with our UK-based mailing house and Our Daily Bread Ministries in the US. We do not sell or share personal information with anyone for marketing purposes.

Please do not complete and sign this form for anyone but yourself. You do not need to complete this form if you already receive regular copies of *Journey Through* from us.

Full Name (Mr/Mrs/Miss/Ms): _____

Address: _____

_____

Postcode: _____ Tel: _____

Email: _____

☐ I would like to receive email updates and details of Our Daily Bread Publishing products.

Signature: _____

All our resources, including *Journey Through*, are available without cost. Many people, making even the smallest of donations, enable Our Daily Bread Ministries to reach others with the life-changing wisdom of the Bible. We are not funded or endowed by any group or denomination.

For information on our resources, visit **ourdailybread.org**. Alternatively, please contact the office nearest you from the list below, or go to **ourdailybread.org/locations** for the complete list of offices.

BELARUS
Our Daily Bread Ministries
PO Box 82, Minsk, Belarus 220107
belarus@odb.org • (375-17) 2854657; (375-29) 9168799

GERMANY
Our Daily Bread Ministries e.V.
Schulstraße 42, 79540 Lörrach
deutsch@odb.org • +49 (0) 7621 9511135

IRELAND
Our Daily Bread Ministries
64 Baggot Street Lower, Dublin 2, D02 XC62
ireland@odb.org • +353 (0) 1676 7315

RUSSIA
MISSION Our Daily Bread
PO Box "Our Daily Bread",
str.Vokzalnaya 2, Smolensk, Russia 214961
russia@odb.org • 8(4812)660849; +7(951)7028049

UKRAINE
Christian Mission Our Daily Bread
PO Box 533, Kiev, Ukraine 01004
ukraine@odb.org • +380964407374; +380632112446

UNITED KINGDOM (Europe Regional Office)
Our Daily Bread Ministries
PO Box 1, Millhead, Carnforth, LA5 9ES
europe@odb.org • +44 (0)15395 64149

ourdailybread.org

Thirsting for more?

Check out **journeythrough.org**

- Find titles available
- Explore other formats:
Read online or receive daily email